Hey Ladies, Stop Apologizing!

... and Other Career Mistakes

V̶̶ ̶M̶a̶k̶e̶

D1369895

Maja Jovanović, Ph.D.
Founder of ALL IN with Prof. Maja

Rock's Mills Press
Oakville, Ontario

PUBLISHED BY

ROCK'S MILLS PRESS

2645 Castle Hill Crescent
Oakville, Ontario L6H 6J1
www.rocksmillspress.com

Photo credits: Valua Vitaly, Shutterstock (p. 175); Maja Jovanović (pp. 176, 177).

Cover design: Jen Harrison I Creative Couture Marketing + Design
www.creativecouturedesign.ca

For information, including bulk orders, permissions requests, and Library and
Archives Canada Cataloguing in Publication data, contact Rock's Mills Press at
customer.service@rocksmillspress.com.

ISBN-13: 978-1-77244-012-6

Dedication

To those who did not think they would succeed.
For those who were afraid—
afraid of failing, afraid of making mistakes,
afraid of questioning the status quo.

And for those who took chances and paved the way. Who chipped
away at barriers, so others could prosper.

Life is better when you believe in yourself,
your vision and your dreams.
Our thoughts do not create our reality;
they are a starting point.
And with unimaginable levels of effort and dedication, great
things can happen for you.

Come to the edge, She said.
They said, We are afraid.
Come to the edge, She said.
They came. She pushed them.
And they flew.

Guillaume Apollinaire

Contents

Preface

Do you doubt yourself or your capabilities? Do you downplay your achievements or refuse to take credit for a job well done? Do you talk yourself out of doing something just so you won't fail? If so, then you've picked up the right book.

Are you always apologizing for things, even when it's not your fault? Are you the type of woman who hates negotiating and will just accept the first offer? Do you dread asking your manager questions or speaking aloud during meetings? Do you think you sound like an idiot when presenting in front of others? Guess what? This book is for you.

Are you a people pleaser, perfectionist and procrastinator? Are you more concerned with keeping the peace than fighting for what's yours?

If so, read on, my friend, READ ON.

I'm so TIRED of hearing women apologize for everything. I'm so OVER listening to women tell me it was *team work* that got the project done instead of their own intelligence and hard work. I'm so SADDENED every time I hear about a woman accepting the first offer of a job without negotiating for more.

I couldn't take it anymore.

I was so OVERWHELMED by all my female students who refuse to ask a question in class or are too scared to meet up with their professors *that I had to do something about it.*

So I started my own company, created a blog (http://allinwithprofmaja.com), founded a social club on campus and wrote a book. (This is the book!)

At first I wondered if these fears surrounding public speaking and this terrible lack of confidence were only a problem for younger women. Then I attended an academic conference that changed my mind forever.

At that conference, I listened to a panel of four *highly* distinguished professors. All were incredibly intelligent, competent women with years of experience in their various fields of sociology, health policy, nutrition and anthropology. The first introduced herself by saying: *"I can't believe I'm sitting on such a distinguished panel with these women, who I've admired my whole life. I don't know what I could possibly add to a discussion that they haven't already written about."*

Um? What?

The audience laughed.

The second woman got up to introduce herself and it's Groundhog Day all over again: *"Well, I feel the same way. I'm so honored to be here with these women, I couldn't even believe they asked me to speak, I thought they sent the email to the wrong person."*

Are you kidding me? Do you sense a pattern here?

Third speaker takes the microphone and adds: *"Oh my goodness, you took the words right out of my mouth. I've been following the work of these women for years, and they're so brilliant, and I'm just so humbled to be sitting here with everyone, I hope I can keep up."*

Oh. My. Goodness.

Last woman gets up to speak.

"Yes, I agree with everyone here. I'm just so grateful to be included among such distinguished speakers. I, too, hope that I'll be as brilliant or thought-provoking as them."

Make this stop. *Please!*

Over the course of this five-day conference I attended at least 25 seminars and *not once*—let me repeat that: *NOT once*—did I hear a man speak in a way that undercut and discredited his experience, knowledge, or level of skill. ***Yet every single time a woman spoke at this conference, an apology was sure to follow.***

I see the same horrifying tendencies that were displayed at this conference on a daily basis in my classrooms and lecture halls, and among my colleagues, friends, neighbors and family members.

That is why I wrote this book.

As women, we must recognize that we have a voice, we have an opinion, and we should know how best to articulate it. We need to know our value, and learn to love the art of self-promotion. We must learn to tame that negative voice in our heads that constantly breeds doubt and fear. We must stop apologizing and start believing we are capable of unimaginable levels of success. We *must* become leaders in all areas of our lives in order to embody and promote that leadership ideal for the generation coming up behind us.

This is what I want you to know: That you can build your self-confidence. You can develop your assertiveness. You can expand out of your comfort zone by taking risks. You can be courageous.

You can be a leader.

You can improve your public speaking skills. You can strengthen the tone of your voice. You can generate charisma and stage presence.

You can stop apologizing.

Please know you are not your mother's disappointment, your guidance counselor's lowered expectations, or the realization of your own failed quest for perfection.

You are not your past, your hurt, your wounds, your trauma or your regrets. You are not the internalized sum of your mistakes; you are not your failures.

Disengage from the endless loop of negative thoughts. Dis-identify from who you thought you were *supposed to be*.

Leave the past alone. There is only . . . *now*. And if you don't start valuing yourself *now*, there will be no future for you.

Begin today. Begin with this book.

And if no one has ever told you before, let me be the first: I believe in you.

How to Use This Book

This is not an academic book. Most academic books are boring, tedious and about 100 pages longer than they need to be. Most people read them only because they're required to and will be tested on the material.

This book may be written by an academic—a sociologist, actually—BUT it's much better. You won't need a dictionary to get through it. You won't be inundated with references to complicated studies and no, you won't be tested on the material.

But if all you do is read this book once, the material will be interesting but ultimately useless. The benefits of this book will be realized only after you've read it a few times, after you've discussed the contents with your friends and colleagues, and after you've spent time thinking about the questions each chapter raises.

Think of it as your guidebook. Here's how to use it.

Begin anywhere you like. You don't need to read the book from start to finish to grasp the essence of what I'm saying. Start in the middle and go backward if you'd like. Or, if you're a Type A nerd like me, you'll start at the preface, read every word from beginning to end, then you'll highlight the important stuff, use sticky notes and write your own notes in the margins. Then you'll photocopy or snap a pic of the cool stuff and send it along to everyone you know who might benefit from some added confidence.

Complete the exercises in the accompanying workbook. Seriously. Do them. Work through them with some patience and honest reflection.

Re-read the sections pertinent to you and where you are in your life right now.

Then PRACTICE. Then DRILL. Then REHEARSE. Then TRAIN. Don't let up. And don't you dare think that you will increase your confidence, improve your speaking or writing skills or learn to love the art of self-promotion without sustained, deliberate, and focused practice.

Then share the knowledge you've gained with EVERY SINGLE woman you know.

Let's do this together.

Introduction

Here's the problem:

- We play nice.
- We don't ask for what we want.
- We don't negotiate.
- We apologize. All. The. Time.
- We're people-pleasers.
- We're over-thinkers.
- We suffer from the imposter syndrome.
- We're perfectionists.
- We don't self-promote.

These internal barriers produce very real financial penalties. By choosing these self-sabotaging behaviors, we opt out of success, out of leadership roles and out of financial security.

This book is about five things: (1) figuring out a vision for your life; (2) working toward your potential; (3) improving your communication skills; (4) increasing your confidence; and (5) avoiding mediocrity.

Who is this book for? My goal with this book is to reach out to women who never thought leadership was possible for them. My mission is to make you aware of your bad habits, to push you out of your comfort zone and into action, and to motivate you to reach UP, to dream bigger, and to aspire to leadership positions in all areas of your life.

Now a shout out to stay-at-home mamas, to mothers transitioning back into the workforce, and to those unsure of their next career step. You may not be able to go ALL IN on certain days because of the competing demands of motherhood or your 9-to-5 job. But this book is still meant for you. Even if right now you can only work on your dreams a few hours a week, keep going, don't stop. A few hours a week is better than none! Those few hours will morph into a more dedicated venture when you decide it's finally time to go ALL IN, ALL THE WAY, ALL THE TIME.

Let this book be the unwavering motivator you need to jump-start the next phase in your life. As you're preparing lunches, cleaning snotty noses, or asking the kiddies for the 17th time to clean up their rooms, please know that you *can* take on a leadership role in any area of your life. Pretend I'm your career BFF and I'm telling you the stuff you really need to know, the stuff no one else is sharing with you.

WHERE DOES MY BOOK FIT?

My philosophy of confidence and empowerment was influenced by many previous writers and thinkers, beginning with Betty Friedan and her famous book, *The Feminine Mystique*. Leslie Bennetts (*The Feminine Mistake*), Judith Warner (*Perfect Madness*), Sharon Hays (*Cultural Contradictions of Motherhood*) and Arlie Russell Hochschild (*The Second Shift*) all have important things to say about the balancing act between motherhood and career. I have to mention the classic *Nice Girls Don't Get the Corner Office* by Lois Frankel. Reading *Lean In* by Sheryl Sandberg was a watershed moment. Then there are communication experts like Judith Humphrey (*Taking the Stage*), procrastination experts like Sam Bennett (*Get It Done*), scholars like Brené Brown (*The Gifts of Imperfection*), negotiation researchers like Linda Babcock and Sara Laschever (*Women Don't Ask*) and Selena Rezvani (*Pushback*), financial gurus like Karen Finerman (*Finerman's Rules*), and finally the newest generation of feminists like Jessica Valenti (*Full Frontal Feminism*).

The difference between these books and mine is that my book discusses the *solutions*, the *strategies*, the *tips* and *tactics* you can use starting TODAY to increase your confidence, improve your communications skills and go ALL IN towards your career.

As women we face a plethora of external barriers, including unequal pay; we also shoulder more than our fair share of responsibility for childcare, pet care, food prep, housework, and all the emotional labor involved in caring for others. We work disproportionately in precarious jobs—short-term, part-time, contract— that pay less and offer fewer benefits. If you're a member of a visible minority, an older woman, or from the LGBTQ community, then your barriers are worse. That's the truth.

I can't solve the problems of discrimination or sexism in the workplace. I can't fix the issues of homophobia or ageism. I acknowledge that these barriers are real, and that they wreak havoc on our lives, but what I *can* help you with is your confidence, your mindset and your communication skills. That's my area of expertise, and that's the point of this book.

Reading this book and completing the exercises in the workbook will be a humbling experience. Perhaps your days aren't as structured as they could be. Perhaps you haven't achieved everything you're capable of, or you don't work as hard or as persistently as you could. Maybe you'll realize you don't take enough risks and playing it safe has hurt your career and your bank account. Perhaps constructive criticism hurts your feelings more than you'd like to admit. But either way, it's finally time to take your career to the next level.

WHAT THIS BOOK IS NOT ABOUT

I will not coddle you. I will not hold your hand and gently tell you you've done a terrific job and it's just the mean, mean world that isn't fair to you. You are *not* a special snowflake. I know you've been told that your whole life, and bless your parents, but it's not true. *Do something special,* then a special snowflake you will be! I will not tell you to burn incense, send positive thoughts out into the universe or be kinder to yourself, while in lotus pose. Nope.

This book will kick your ass! It will force you to look at the ugly truth that is your current work ethic, your schedule, and your lack of vision and commitment. This book will drag the excuses out of you, and ask you: Are you working to your fullest potential? Can you do more? And the answer is YES. Yes, you can. You can always do more.

As women we are capable of SO much more than we're actually doing every day, and what we think we can do.

We must advance. We must conquer our internal demons. And I'm here to help.

Let us be bold. Let us begin today.

We must get out of our own way. Get out of our minds. Get out of our thoughts. We must step aside and do the friggin' work. We must commit every SINGLE day to the work necessary to ensure our own success and the success of our families. We need to be confident, articulate and successful role models for our daughters, our sisters, our mothers, our neighbors and strangers alike.

Why shouldn't WE be in leadership positions? Why shouldn't WE push forward our ideas, our game plan, and our initiatives? Why shouldn't WE apply for that promotion?

Why not you? Why not me?

Stop waiting for permission and take ownership of your life.

Let us rise UP towards leadership.

Let us believe we are worthy and capable of extreme, extraordinary levels of success and then outwork our competition.

Success does not just happen. We create it. We harness it, we develop it and we make it our own.

It's time, ladies. It's time.

Every time a woman
stands up for herself,
without knowing it,
possibly without
claiming it,
she stands up for all
women.

—*Dr. Maya Angelou,*
poet, writer, activist

1

The
ALL
IN
Vision

What's the Problem?
Lack of Women Leaders!

Sadly, men still run the world, in business, finance, science, technology, entrepreneurial start-ups, restaurants, and entertainment.... You get the idea.

Only 17 out of 195 independent countries are run by women.

In the U.S. 50% of college graduates are women, BUT the very top leadership positions are still held almost exclusively by men.

Only 21% of Fortune 500 CEOs are women.[1]

In the U.S., white women hold 14% of executive officer positions, while women of color hold 4% (!) of top corporate jobs. White women hold 17% of board seats, while women of color hold 3%. White women hold 18% of congressional seats, women of color only 5%.

As of 2010, women in the U.S. made 77 cents for every dollar a man made. If you were an African-American woman, you only made 65 cents, and Latina women made only 56 cents for every dollar earned by a non-Latino man.[2]

In Canada, women are outpacing men in higher education: 55% of students are women, 45% men. BUT there are still major gender differences in the type of degrees earned: 18% of computer science degrees go to women. Only 24% of engineering degrees are earned by women.

We also know that women are more likely to work in precarious jobs, where part-time, casual, contract work equals less pay, fewer benefits, and no job stability or security.

Only 16% of the directors of Canadian companies are women. More than 40% of Canadian companies had NO women directors on their boards (!).[3]

Affordability and availability of daycare are a major issue for women and a reason why so many women are working part-time.

Most childcare, household chores and meal preparation are still done by women. But women can't do it all! —We can't take care of the home, the groceries, the nutrition, the children, our partners and pets, volunteer, spend time with friends *and* have stimulating full-time careers.

If they can't see it, they can't dream it. If women don't see other women in positions of power and authority, in real leadership roles, then it's difficult to envision themselves as leaders. This lack of female role models is pervasive. For instance, the Academy Award-winning actress Geena Davis founded the Geena Davis Institute on Gender in Media to investigate gender bias in the entertainment field.[4] Her research revealed that only 23% of films feature a female protagonist. Only 21% of film-makers are women. Women are shown in sexually revealing clothing twice as often as men. Men are cast in on-screen STEM (science, technology, engineering and math) career roles seven times as often as women (!!)[5]

What do movies teach girls about the working world? Well, 80% of male movie characters work (i.e., hold a job or profession), while only 20% of women are shown in a job-related manner.[6] Those female characters who do work are more often depicted in stereotypical roles (waitress, teacher), and NOT ONE female in the 21 films analyzed held a medical, scientific, executive or political role. Not one! The majority of all business owners, soldiers and police officers in films are men.

The more girls watch such stereotyped portrayals in the movies and on TV, the more they come to believe that women have very restricted options for employment.[7] As a result, we continue to live in a world dominated by male stories, male protagonists, male voices and male opinions.

I struggle with this onslaught of male leadership roles in children's books and cartoons. I ONLY purchase books with a female lead character, and those can be difficult to find. I never read my daughter books that end with a woman needing a man to save her, rescue her or love her. I make a very deliberate (and time-consuming) effort to enforce the idea that others do not complete her; she must complete herself. So we read *Rosie Revere, Engineer*[8] instead of books about princesses. And every time she tells me she wants to be a princess when she grows up, I ask: "Ryo, why doesn't Mama like princesses?" And she responds, "Because princesses don't have jobs and they always need someone to help them."

Damn right! I'm raising a LEADER and it starts when they're toddlers. Every single day I reinforce the fact that leadership positions are always an option for her if she works hard.

SOME SOLUTIONS

- *We need affordable nationwide childcare,* so every child (regardless of their parents' finances) can receive high quality care and their mamas can go back to work and not have their income interruption affect their long-term financial stability.[9] The longer a woman is out of the workforce on maternity leave (paid or not paid), the less money she makes long-term.[10,11]
- *We need gender equity in the education system (including books),* so that girls are encouraged, supported and mentored to take science, technology, engineering and math.
- *We need equal levels of financial support for women-led companies, not just start-ups.*[3]
- Most importantly, *we need more girls and more women of all ages who dream of leadership positions, who want to be leaders, and who see themselves as smart enough and capable enough to be in positions of power.*

We need women to know leadership is an option for them. Women don't need to spend their lives working in the lower tiers of organizations or in middle management. We can reach UP. We can dream bigger. We can work harder. We can help each other. We need women to *want* to be the decision-makers. We need more women leaders. Full stop.

This starts with you going ALL IN.

The ALL IN Mindset

ALL IN is a mindset that forces you to discard your excuses and live up to your potential. Follow the rules below to start embodying the characteristics of successful people who go ALL IN, ALL THE WAY, ALL THE TIME:

1. **Create a vision for your life.** If you don't know what you're working towards, then you're working on someone else's dream, not your own. Take five minutes right now and write down your vision for your life. It must be clear, focused and quantifiable. Wanting to "make a difference in the world" doesn't count, because it's too generic and besides, everyone says that. Your vision needs to be specific: *I want to get into medical school so I can become a surgeon to help cancer patients like my mom.* Or, *I want to become a leading expert on LGBTQ issues to bring attention to the inequalities they encounter.* You've got to be specific. Write down your vision, say it aloud and then make sure everything you do moves you closer to achieving this vision.

2. **Success is maximizing your potential.** Success is not about obtaining a degree, a job or a new title. Do you have a B.A.? So what? Did you reach your potential? Have you started a new job? So what? Did you reach your potential? Success is a dynamic state of mind that forces you to ask yourself: *Can I do more? Can I achieve more?* And the answer is always YES. Yes, you can. Make the first move, read this book, do the workbook exercises and I'll get you there.

3. **ACT NOW.** Learn to work with the pressure and necessity of NOW. What can you do NOW? Not tomorrow, not next Monday, not next month—but now. What can you do now to achieve your potential? Now.

4. **Get comfortable with being uncomfortable.** The #1 thing you must sacrifice in order to achieve greatness is your obsession with being comfortable. Get used to the butterflies, the nervousness, the anxiety, and the stress. Because if you're not uncomfortable, you're not taking enough risk in your life.

5. **Beware of mediocrity.** If you're not EXCEPTIONAL in your work ethic, your dedication and your passion, then you're mediocre. You might as well find some 9-to-5 job that you can punch in and out of. Mediocrity is all around you. If you're not phenomenal or remarkable in what you're doing, then you're doing something wrong.

As an example, here's how I try to remain ALL IN throughout the day:

- **Every single day I re-read my vision.** "I want to help women become leaders in all areas of their lives through effective communication and confidence-building strategies. I want to encourage more women to reach for and attain leadership positions, especially those women who never thought it possible, through better communication and self-promotion skills."
- **I time-block my most important tasks.** From 9:30 a.m. till noon I work on what NEEDS to be done (not the easiest stuff). I turn OFF technology. I turn off my email alerts and text messages. I don't answer the phone if it rings. I don't leave my room unless it's for the bathroom.
- **I read inspiring material all the time**, to keep me motivated when the going gets ROUGH. I've reread Steven Pressfield's books (*The War of Art; Turning Pro; Do the Work*) dozens of times.
- **I get comfortable with the messiness of life.** Since I work from home I have to get used to seeing dishes in the sink, my daughter's playroom being a disaster and three loads of laundry waiting to be put away. At times, that laundry doesn't move for two days. Oh well. I get used to it.
- **I hold myself accountable** by scoring my daily productivity (see the productivity template on page 45).

When You Don't Know
What to Do with Your Life

Listen, it's OK if you don't know what you want to do immediately after graduating. Most people don't, myself included. All I knew during my undergraduate days was that I loved public speaking and my writing skills were getting better. But I had NO idea what I wanted to do with my life.

Not knowing what you want to do right away isn't a problem. *The problem is following other people's dreams instead of your own.* We frequently internalize parental expectations (e.g., you must be a doctor, lawyer, or engineer) or peer influences ("Let's backpack across Europe!"), and, before you know it, you've found yourself doing something you hate and you don't even know how you got there.

Figure out what you want to do by listening to yourself more often. (Easier said than done, right?)

Please know that there's no perfect answer for what you should do after you graduate. I don't have the answer and neither does anyone else. There is no single path for you. You'll take multiple paths down roads you never thought you'd be on, and you'll be fine as long as you're open to taking risks and going beyond your comfort zone.

The most important thing you can do as you figure out your vision for your life is to learn something new. You must acquire new skills and never stop learning in whatever job you take after school. Each job doesn't have to be "THE JOB"—the perfect job in the perfect industry with the perfect salary—BUT each job should provide you with an opportunity for growth. Otherwise, why would you stay there?

As long as you're learning and challenging yourself you'll eventually figure out how to align your vision for your life with your daily goals.

TIPS

- *Welcome uncertainty* and go with it. Nobody has it all figured out all of the time.
- *Beware of perfectionism.* It can creep up in all areas of your life.
- *Recognize the internalized gendered norms ALL AROUND YOU.* Are you socialized to be helpful, a nurturer, to be nice, friendly, and a people-pleaser?
- Whatever job you're contemplating taking, ask yourself: *What can I learn in this job?* What new skills can I acquire? Is this job challenging? Will I be able to grow?
- It's never about achieving one skill at a time, but rather *building a skill set and working towards your ultimate vision*, which will become clearer along the way.

Where's Your Fire?

Where's your fire, your passion? What makes you jump out of bed at 5 a.m.?

If your dreams feel like work, then you're doing the wrong work.

Working on fulfilling your dreams should be stressful . . . BUT a good stress. You must distinguish between a stress that invigorates you and a stress that depresses you.

I can't give you passion, or tell you where to find it. I can only emphasize that without passion you're probably fulfilling someone else's dreams.

Your passion should be a way of life; it should be ingrained in your daily regime, your habits, your intuition, and your disposition.

If you think success is only an option then you're doing the wrong work, you're in the wrong career; you're on the wrong path.

People who complain that they don't know what to do are often just confused, so they drift from course to course, job to job without ever realizing what they want in life. That was me at some point in my life—probably all of us.

Treat every job as an opportunity to learn something new. Learn new skills, challenge yourself and then move onto another job. And if you're not working right now, or you're a stay-at-home mom, what can you do to fire up that passion?

Here's a list of everything that I tried during my LONG years as a student:

- Tried being a waitress but only lasted through the orientation, because the manager tried to hit on me and it made me feel gross. I walked right on outta there and applied for a retail position selling jeans. Didn't like that either. Lasted two shifts.
- Worked as an administrative assistant in an office (handling paperwork, photocopying, answering phones, dealing with the public).
- Worked in retail sales, selling high-end fitness equipment.

- Volunteered for Hospice Toronto, where I worked with the dying for four hours every week. I did this for 10 years! I wrote my Master's thesis on hospice care and then got a book deal to publish my memoir on working with the dying.
- Worked as a self-taught makeup artist for various brands at Holt Renfrew (Bobbi Brown makeup, NARS, Laura Mercier) and also for MAC; then worked in a beauty boutique at Shoppers Drug Mart.
- Became a research assistant and worked on the following topics: gambling, Aboriginal health, Aboriginal gambling, traumatic brain injuries, editing undergraduate textbooks, eco-conscious consumer trends, homelessness and addiction issues.
- Became a teaching assistant for various sociology courses.

I worked in malls and little boutiques; I worked in offices and from home. I worked for one boss and a team of leaders. I worked for men and women. I worked with only men at some jobs and only women at others. I worked crazy shift-work and part-time hours (they're the worst!). I worked nights (4 p.m. to midnight), split shifts (two hours in the morning then back for three hours in the afternoon—again, it's the worst!).

> **Part of finding your passion is figuring out what you do NOT like to do.**

Throughout all of these opportunities I learned a tremendous amount about what I enjoyed doing, and also about what I definitely did NOT want to do with my life. But in each job I learned a new skill (whether that was a new software program, bettering my public speaking, or just getting more comfortable with rejection—which happens all the time in retail).

So my advice to you is to get out there and try as many different things as you can. Fail often and you'll figure out where your talents lie, and where your passion catches fire. Take a risk. Get out of your comfort zone. Keep asking yourself what you would do with your life if you weren't afraid. Answer that question and you'll find your passion.

TIPS

- *Take on new opportunities.* Work in different areas and try everything at least once. Work in an office (in a cubicle), work for an entrepreneur, work in the business, entertainment or fashion industry. Intern for a non-profit, volunteer doing something totally out-of-the-box (I worked with the dying as a hospice volunteer for 10 years—a total out-of-the-box experience that I never imagined doing).

- *Stop chasing the perfect job and focus on learning new skills.* Each and every job you have should be an opportunity to LEARN SOMETHING NEW. I must shout this at you, because so often new graduates are obsessed (and stressed out) about finding the perfect job, with the perfect company. Do not fall for this trap. And don't believe you'll make $80,000 in your first job out of school. It won't happen. So, focus on what new skills you'll be learning in your job. How can you be challenged in your job?

- *Recognize there's no one correct pathway to find your passion.* Unless you're one of those really lucky people who knew since they were five years old what they wanted to be and absolutely nothing or nobody stood in their way. For the rest of us, it takes a little time and a lot of different experiences to figure it out, and that's OK.

- *Start listening to yourself and stop listening to what others think you should be doing with your life.* Maybe you need to tune out your parents, friends and your internal negative voice, and start focusing on what gives you joy.

What's Your Vision?

What is your vision for your life? How will you achieve it? Your vision anchors your daily and weekly goals and ensures you achieve them. Without a long-term vision, it's easy to get side-tracked by cute animal videos on YouTube or indulge in a five-hour Netflix bender of *Downton Abbey*, *Suits*, *Scandal*, or *How to Get Away with Murder*. OK, you get the idea! We've all been there, but now we need to change.

Be clear and focused about what you want. Your vision (or dream, calling, destiny, or whatever you want to label it) should be SKY HIGH and challenging enough to make you uncomfortable. When you envision the greatest life possible for yourself, what does it look like? To borrow some famous questions from Stanislavsky (an old-school acting coach):

- Who are you?
- What do you want?
- Why do you want it?
- How will you achieve your goals?
- What must you overcome?

Never doubt the importance of writing your vision down. Unless you do, you're hostage to chance, to dreams, hopes and intentions. This will be the manifesto of your life. And without a written manifesto to reinforce your daily intentions you will be distracted. You will follow the herd and conform to the "norm." Figuring out your vision is arduous and ego-bruising. It is not for amateurs. It takes time and thoughtful reflection.

> **If your dream only includes you, it's too small.**
> —*Ava Du Vernay, director of Selma*

Your vision should be meaningful and authentic for you. It should also be a *stretch*, meaning it's not something that's easily achieved.

Establishing a focused vision ensures that your daily activity is always aligned with your long-term goals. Simply put, if you don't take daily consistent action towards your vision, you will never achieve what you want.

STEPS TO CREATING YOUR VISION

- Write down everything you've ever wanted in your life. The career you want, the salary you need, the places you want to live or visit, the schedule you prefer, the level of fitness you need to make you happy, and so on.
- What brings you joy? What have you always wanted to do? What activities make you happy? How can you link these to your career?
- Narrow down these aspirational projects to your top five projects and goals.
- Now, which one of your top five goals would you regret most if you didn't achieve? Pick ONE.
- Then, further narrow your vision into a one- to two-sentence statement that accurately reflects what you want from life, based on your top goal.
- Tell someone your vision. How do they react? Supportive or are they a hater? Learn to embrace the support and discard the hate. It's that simple.

Here's my vision statement:

I want to help women gain leadership positions in any area of their lives by bettering their communication and self-promotion skills.

And here are a few others:

- The Khan Academy: *To provide a free world-class education to anyone anywhere.*
- Patagonia: *Build the best product, cause no unnecessary harm, use business to inspire and implement solutions to the environmental crisis.*
- *Martha Stewart Living* magazine: Martha Stewart Living *teaches consumers how to elevate the everyday and special occasions confidently, creatively, and beautifully.*

What Are Your Goals?

Forget about setting reasonable goals. Save that for those who settle for mediocrity. You need EXTREME goals to push you right out of your comfort zone.

If you're going to push past procrastination or resistance, you'll need some extraordinary payoff to get you there. If you're going to maintain the energy, stamina and determination to get to the top, the rewards better be phenomenal. So, reach UP. Demand more of yourself.

Eleven months ago my blog didn't exist. Now I've written over 200 posts! I finished a book in five months (plus another six months for edits and revisions), started a social club on campus, and posted 33 YouTube videos (OK, I know, I need to work on those videos. . . . I will, I promise!).

I gave myself the goal of writing five blog posts a day and posting one video a day on YouTube. Sure, I didn't always hit my targets, but I did a hell of a lot better than I would have if I'd set lower goals.

Start with small goals and sadly you might just stay small.

I push myself so damn hard (and I still have my regular research gig and teaching and a spouse and raising a toddler and looking after a dog) because my goals are so damn ambitious.

You should have goals for all areas of your life: your career, fitness, financial, relationships and friendships, and your emotional and spiritual well-being. *WRITE YOUR GOALS DOWN.* Every night, review your goals for the next day. Ask yourself how you scored today and how you can improve tomorrow.

The goals you set will help structure your daily to-do list.

What are YOUR goals? How far have you stretched yourself? How many risks have you taken to get to the NEXT level?

To give you an example, here are some of my goals:

- My blog generates one million views per month
- I earn $25,000 from on-line advertising
- I give five paid public talks per week.
- I own five apartment complexes that generate income
- I have no consumer debt.
- I write one book a year.
- My books are *New York Times* best-sellers.
- I've given two TED Talks.
- I consider Sheryl Sandberg, Amy Schumer and Serena Williams mentors of mine.
- I run four half-marathons a year.
- My personal best half-marathon time is 1 hour, 29 minutes.
- I have a healthy and thriving marriage and family.
- I have $150,000 saved up for my daughter's education.
- I have over 100 people working for me who love their work.
- I have a million followers on my YouTube channel.

Do you see what I mean?

Clearly I haven't achieved these goals, but damn, how crappy would my life be if I didn't dream big—if I didn't have INTENSE goals to keep pushing me?

Now it's your turn.

Never Lower Your Goals

When you don't achieve your goals, do you think it's all right to lower them? Women have internalized failure; we're so worried we're going to fail that we lower our goals until we've convinced ourselves we didn't want to achieve them in the first place.

When I started my website my goal was 35 blog postings per week. After two weeks, I didn't make that goal, but I did write 55 posts! Can you imagine if my original goal had been only one post a day, or seven per week? Playing it safe gets you nowhere.

We have to stretch our goals beyond our comfort zone, because we will fail at some point. You'll never complete everything on your to-do list every single day.

> **If you place limits on your potential, you will limit your ability to be successful.**

Why aim for mediocrity, when you know mediocrity doesn't get rewarded?

This is especially a problem for women because we don't speak up unless we're certain we have the right answer. We don't try something twice if we've failed at it the first time. We don't work on our weaknesses because we think we should be perfect and flawless and have everything all figured out.

Lower your goals and you're lowering your standard of living. I'm serious. If we don't get more women to dream bigger, aspire to be more and achieve more, we will continue to be the ones who follow orders, instead of being the decision makers.

This. Is. The. Truth.

HOW TO ENSURE YOU KEEP YOUR GOALS

STEP 1: *Write* your goals down.
STEP 2: *Commit* by telling others your goals.
STEP 3: *Be accountable* by sending progress reports to others and keep regular score of yourself.

Psychologist Gail Matthew's research[12] shows that people who write their goals down are significantly more likely to achieve them. People who share their goals with others and are held accountable by progress reports are (you guessed it) MORE likely to stay committed.

Making a public declaration of your goals forces you to be (held) accountable.

How Badly Do You Want Success?

Some people want success, but they only want to work for it part-time. Some people need success like they need air to breathe.

Do you need success so badly that you feel you're suffocating in your daily life? Or are you like most people and you sort-of-only-really want a little bit of success?

Maybe you're one of those people who dreams of being successful but does nothing about achieving it. Maybe you're stunningly successful IN YOUR MIND, yet never translate that into daily consistent ACTION.

Maybe you envy the lifestyles of successful people who don't have to look at the price tags of items and can afford to go to Starbucks twice a day and wear designer suits. . . .

> **Everybody wants to be famous, but nobody wants to do the work.**
> —*Kevin Hart,*
> *comedian*

Maybe you like the look of successful people flying in first class with their Louis Vuitton handbags and Louboutin heels, but it never occurred to you to bust your ass working non-stop to achieve those things.

I'll ask you again: How badly do you want success? Can you describe what success means to you?

How prepared are you to work every single day, day after day, month after month . . . and NEVER let up, in order to fulfill your dreams?

It's so tough, it's so exhausting, and the rejection can sometimes be both debilitating and depressing. But the alternative is always SO much worse. The alternative is mediocrity.

Remember, the alternative to success is mediocrity. The alternative to achieving phenomenal levels of success is maintaining the status quo . . . doing the same old thing you're doing already and getting nowhere . . . living pay check to pay check, counting your nickels and clipping coupons and looking for the sales.

That kind of life has to be WORSE than working your ass off to achieve your fullest potential.

It just has to be.

Don't be one of those people who always *talks* about being an artist, designer, creator, writer, actor, graduate student, lawyer, comedian—but then never actually designs, creates or writes anything.

Talent is not enough.

Intelligence alone will not guarantee success.

Timing helps, but only a little.

Experience is useful, but not always a requirement.

But the one thing that is not negotiable is HARD WORK. Without an obsessive level of determination and mind-numbing effort you will not succeed. You won't even come close.

You can always do more.

Start today. Start now.

Act Now

Do you ever get energized about starting something new, only to put it off? Do you procrastinate? Forget about time management. What you need to do *right now* is ACT. Take action today, not tomorrow.

People complain all the time about not having enough money, hating the job they're in, or not being fit enough, yet they don't do anything about it right away. They don't take immediate action. They just think about it.

You want to get into better shape? Stop thinking about it, stop browsing Pinterest and Instagram for that "perfect body"—which doesn't exist, by the way—and get on the floor and do 25 push-ups, right now. Hold a plank position for 30 seconds. ACT NOW.

Hate your job? Want a different career? Why wait until Monday? Start now. Be accountable. Call 10 potential employers and ask for an interview!

The problem is, people aren't willing to sacrifice their comfort zone to try something different and change their lives RIGHT NOW. They want to, they dream about it, they talk about it, they even envision it. But putting out "positive energy" into the world is not going to get you a different life. You need to work, and work harder than you've ever worked before. Take your work ethic to the EXTREME.

Students always complain to me about not being happy with their writing abilities or their lack of critical thinking, and I always ask them the same question: *WHAT ARE YOU DOING ABOUT IT RIGHT NOW?*

I have one student who wasn't the best writer, and then she came to me for help. She started seeing me regularly during office hours. She got books out of the library on grammar, writing style, and critical thinking. She went to the writing lab on campus for help. She practiced and practiced and practiced. And where she is today is so far from where she was two years ago, because during that two years she worked consistently on bettering her writing skills. And now she has even published her work in a local paper.

That's what you need to do. ACT with intensity, with purpose and with passion. Never, ever put off your dreams until tomorrow. Don't start on a Monday what you can start now. NOW!

Act now, and follow up that action with more action, immediately.

TIPS

- Name one person who could help you with your vision. (Maybe you need their advice, mentorship, a coffee break with them for inspiration. Or maybe you just need them to be a sounding board for your ideas.)
- Name someone who will definitely *not* help you with your goal. (Maybe this person is a family member, spouse or friend. It doesn't mean you need to block their number and avoid them, but perhaps you need to minimize the time you spend with them while you finish your project. If they sap you of energy and don't inspire you, reconsider spending your free time with them for now.)

Now, what ONE goal will you take action on today?

Manage Your Time

How you structure your time, who you hang out with, what you listen to and read, what influences you—all these choices must be highly strategic in order for you to navigate the road to success.

If you want success (and I mean *unbelievable amounts of success*), you need to be strategic. You need to plan the work and work the plan.

You must be strategic in dealing with negative influences around you, or you'll start doubting yourself.

You must be strategic in dealing with that inner voice that always whispers that you can't do something, that you're not smart enough or good enough. If you don'T SHUT THAT INNER VOICE DOWN it will ruin your life because it will keep you from believing in yourself and pushing yourself to be more productive.

> **You must be strategic with your time or time will control you and your results.**

You must be strategic in what you watch, the news you follow, the books you read, and the people you spend time with. Or else you'll waste your life on meaningless trivia, and toxic relationships, instead of actively investing in your career.

Strategies are tied to your goals, and if you don't have a goal you can BET that you're working on someone else's goal. You're helping someone else achieve success, while only dreaming of success for yourself.

Start each day strategically. Live each day authentically. *And ask yourself: Am I busy or am I productive?* A lifetime can be wasted on being busy *and* bored.

You should NEVER start your day not knowing what your daily goals are or how they align with your ultimate vision.

Begin each day by reviewing your vision and writing down your daily goals. Then take action. Stop over-thinking everything and start taking deliberate and focused action on ONE thing to move you forward. What's the most important ONE thing you can do?

Be strategic in every single thing you do. Having a strategy gives order to your day; it motivates you to keep going when the long-term payoff is still too far away for you to see. Being strategic helps keep you organized and on track for success.

End each day by answering these questions:

- *Was my day meaningful?*
- *Was I productive or merely busy?*
- *What did I learn?*
- *What did I create?*
- *What did I truly accomplish today?*
- *Did I move my career forward today?*

Answering these questions will force you to be more accountable for your days and how your time is spent.

Visualize Success

Wherever you are in life, you must make a commitment to win, to see yourself crossing the finish line in first place. You must visualize success before you can achieve success.

Part of this visualization process is forgetting what you don't have—enough time, money, support, staff, resources, experience, etc.—and concentrating with complete tunnel vision on your *strengths.*

You will NEVER have it all perfectly in place. Life is messy. Who has all the time, experience, money and resources? No one. We could all use more of everything. Therefore, you've got to start somewhere. Start where you are right now.

Forget your weaknesses and believe that all of your skills, talents, experiences, passion, enthusiasm, drive, talent and dedication will be enough—will get you started.

If you don't believe you can do something and be successful right now with what you have today, you'll always depend on excuses: *"Oh, I didn't have enough money or experience or time to do X or Y or Z."*

No more excuses.

No more wasted time.

Stop lying to yourself about why you haven't achieved success. Your perfectionism is tied to fear and by letting go of your perfectionism, you can finally start taking chances and figuring things out as you go along. Remember too that figuring things out as you go is fine. Letting go of perfectionism is freedom. —It's freedom to try things and fail and try again. It's freedom to speak up, lean in and ask for what you want. Freedom to be yourself and not who others want you to be.

Let go of perfectionism and you'll start feeling free.

Visualize yourself as successful and then start acting. Start working on your dreams today. Don't wait for tomorrow—that's what day-dreamers do. They live in their minds without exerting any kind of effort at changing their lives for the better.

Part of the visualization of success is the ***visualization of the process of success.*** This means you must start visualizing the steps needed to get you from A to B. *How* will you succeed? *How* will you achieve greatness? *How* will you win?

Act now. Visualize success.

You must decide your legacy.

Are you a do-er? Will you act? Will you create?

Or—

Will you spectate? Will you sit on the sidelines, seething with jealousy and regret, envious that others are doing what you're too scared to do for yourself?

You decide.

True or False Quiz:
Are You Fulfilling Your Potential?

Answer true or false to the following questions to evaluate your areas for improvement.

1.	I don't internalize my failures or mistakes.	T	F
2.	I ignore that negative voice in my mind.	T	F
3.	The people I spend time with have huge goals and dreams for themselves.	T	F
4.	I am prepared to do anything necessary to achieve my vision (for example, outwork everyone).	T	F
5.	I minimize negative influences in my life (people, TV, internet, movies, music, etc.).	T	F
6.	I read one book a week.	T	F
7.	I try to learn something new in each opportunity or situation.	T	F
8.	I take constructive criticism well.	T	F
9.	I'm always looking forward, not worrying about past events or failures.	T	F
10.	I try to please myself first, not others.	T	F
11.	I speak up often.	T	F
12.	Change excites me.	T	F
13.	I enjoy networking wherever possible.	T	F
14.	I often tell others about my vision or dream for myself.	T	F
15.	When I don't do well on something I seek constructive feedback.	T	F
16.	I speak to my professors and/or managers on a regular basis.	T	F
17.	I feel comfortable speaking aloud and voicing my opinion at school or work.	T	F
18.	I have a system in place for when I fail at something.	T	F
19.	Every day I have goals in place that are aligned with my ultimate vision.	T	F
20.	I love challenges.	T	F
21.	I try to take risks whenever possible.	T	F

22.	I force myself out of my comfort zone on a regular basis.	T	F
23.	When I do something I commit ALL THE WAY.	T	F
24.	I am goal-oriented.	T	F
25.	I am highly motivated to achieve my fullest potential every single day.	T	F
26.	I don't lower my expectations, I dream big!	T	F
27.	I am not a perfectionist.	T	F
28.	I regularly hang out with people who are more successful than me.	T	F
29.	I constantly evaluate myself to see where I can improve.	T	F
30.	I support and encourage other women to go ALL IN.	T	F
31.	I am not a people pleaser.	T	F
32.	My schedule is organized and efficient.	T	F
33.	I don't waste time on Netflix benders or browsing the Web.	T	F
34.	I regularly invest in my career (e.g., attending seminars, reading, networking).	T	F

How many TRUE answers do you have?

0–9	Damn, girl. Thank goodness you're looking for help!
10–19	OK, you need to create some daily structure and develop an ultimate vision for your life.
20–25	Definitely room for improvement.
25–34	Whoa, superstar! You could lead a master class on female empowerment!

I say if I'm beautiful.
I say if I'm strong.
You will NOT determine
my story—I will.

—Amy Schumer,
comedienne

2

Barriers

Barrier #1
Time Scheduling

Say yes, and you'll figure it out afterwards.

—*Tina Fey, actress, comedienne, author*

It may seem like everything is chipping away at your time. At the end of the day you're exhausted but unproductive. Learn how to own your time.

Time Management

My friends always ask me for tips on time management. Every year it's the top issue students deal with. So, how do you manage your time better?

Start TAKING action, stop THINKING about your course of action. It's literally that simple.

I could end the chapter now, but I'll indulge this issue a bit further.

Most people waste their time because:

- *They dabble.* They dabble a little here, they try something over there, and they just coast from course-to-course or house-chore to house-chore or job-to-job without ever establishing a vision (i.e., an ultimate dream to work toward). Without that vision, you easily waste your time. Dabbling also prevents you from going ALL IN because you're straddling two different worlds, not ready to drop the safety net, take a risk and go ALL IN. You can spend months, even years of your life just drifting along, going nowhere.

- *They're reactive, not proactive.* Instead of merely reacting to events in your life—deadlines, projects and assignments—you need to assume initiative and steer your career and your life in the direction you want.

- *They lack an overall vision for their lives.* Forget about reading time management books or attending seminars on how to manage your time better. What you need to figure out is the vision for your life. Where do you see yourself? What does success look like for you? What brings you joy? How much money would make you happy? Establish a vision that is focused and quantifiable (that way, you can evaluate yourself) and you'll start managing your time better.

- *There's no sense of urgency.* People act as if time is unlimited—as if they have their whole lives to be productive and successful. But you don't. Success does not happen over-night; it happens after incredible amounts of daily, consistent effort and planning. And then, add a few years to that.

- *People underestimate the work needed to create success.* If you've underestimated how difficult it will be to achieve success, then you're more likely to let failure stop you. BUT if you already know and are prepared to work five times as hard to achieve your success, then you expect failure and work around it. See the difference? Successful people learn from their failures and move forward because they know failure is part of the process, whereas unsuccessful people are thrown off course by their failures and mistakes and then they just stop. And. Do. Nothing. At. All. *Voilà!* Procrastination sets in.

Make time work for you. Don't be owned by time.

Take immediate action today. Make sure you do something today to move yourself forward.

EXERCISE

There are 168 hours in a week. Where does your time go?

Activity	Hours Per Day	Hours Per Week
Sleeping		
Getting ready for work		
Exercise		
Eating		
Food preparation (grocery shopping, meal preparation, etc.)		
Typical work day/week		
Commuting		
Childcare		
Pet care		
Running errands (miscellaneous)		
Time with friends and family		
Using technology (TV, tablet, phone, etc.)		
Anything else you do		
Other		

Punctuality

Always be on time. Better yet, be early.

Never, ever arrive late to anything, whether it be professional, academic, business, family, friends, or social. It's just rude and disrespectful, and frankly, no one cares about the traffic or construction or road closures or GPS glitches. All they care about is that you're late. You didn't care enough to get organized and be on time. That's what people remember, not the excuses.

Respect people's time, don't waste it. Plan for your meeting to run a bit late, plan to have to put gas in the car or stop for a coffee fix. Build these things into your schedule.

Being late is a character flaw, and people will be less inclined to work with you or hang out with you if you're not reliable and dependable.

If you're not 15 minutes early, you're late. Enough said.

You Can't Do Everything

Why are you trying to do it all? You can't. No one can. Not everything can be a priority. Not everything can be completed today.

Can you just do less stuff?

Seriously, do you have to do it all?

No, you don't.

So, remove one thing from your to-do list.

What can you outsource? Is there someone who can help, (a spouse, partner, parents, family, friends, colleagues, neighbors, or hired help)?

OR could this item just not get done? OR not get such a large investment of your time?

Listen, you can't have a Martha Stewart-inspired house, Goop-caliber recipes, locally harvested organic food, plus take care of your family, run errands, look after the pets, do the car pool, make the dentist appointments, go to work, exercise, make time for your spouse and—oh yeah— work on your career (!) all at the same time.

I have been that women who tried to do it all. And I have been that woman crying on my kitchen floor, cooking six dishes, reading my emails and vacuuming while at the same time organizing a play-date for my toddler. I've been that woman doing the drop-offs and pick-ups from daycare, walking the dog, cleaning the house, cooking the friggin' meals, and then trying to find the inspiration and motivation (and energy!) to sit down and write something brilliant and useful. It's impossible. Perfectionism hurts. It steals away your ambition because EVERY damn day your schedule is impossible to handle, so every day you feel like a failure.

And I *still* suffer from this. I still battle with this culturally ingrained idea that mothering will be a seamlessly glorious experience while simultaneously pursuing a competitive career and sexually adventurous marriage, ALL while having enough time to chat on the phone and catch up with friends for lattés.

But after enough tears on the kitchen floor, I've learned we need to pick our battles. Maybe the house is messier. Maybe you order take-out instead of cooking gourmet meals. Maybe the kids have to kick it up a notch and help out around the house. You've got to find some short cuts, bend the rules, buy the cakes for school, and don't bake them. Maybe you can't make every hockey game, ballet class or music lesson.

Maybe you have to prioritize your career. Maybe, just maybe, *you need to PRIORITIZE YOUR CAREER!*

If you don't work on your craft, if you don't consciously and deliberately work toward your ultimate vision for your life EVERY SINGLE DAY, you will never succeed. But hey, at least you drove the kids to school, right? At least you cooked some meals. Who cares about your pension, or the fact that you get passed over for promotions, or you're not yet financially independent.

You can't do it all. So what do you want to do?

To-Do List vs. Priority List

A to-do list is usually a scattered long-ass list of errands and appointments pulling you in many different directions while seemingly everything on your list screams "Look at me! I'm an emergency! If you don't complete me I'll ruin your life!"

Your to-do list creates a sense of panic because it just keeps growing and you never complete everything you want to on any given day. F**– your to-do list. Seriously. Listen to me: Do everything on your to-do list and you'll go nowhere. You will go *nowhere*.

Your PRIORITY LIST, however, is like a "success list" or a "victory list." It keeps you focused on the KEY one or two things that *matter* most, not whatever screams at you the loudest.

Complete your PRIORITY LIST first and you'll get closer to fulfilling your ultimate vision for yourself, one three-hour block at a time. That's 21 hours a week devoted to your career, and that's an awesome start.

Remember, not everything can be completed, not everything matters equally, and not everything demands your attention RIGHT NOW. Prioritize. Focus. Always remember the bigger picture, and the reason you're willing to put in the late nights, early mornings and sacrifice your social life and finances in order to succeed in the long run.

Never, ever prioritize your to-do list over your priority list. Most importantly, make your priority list happen by incorporating TIME-BLOCKING every single day. (More in the next chapter on that.)

On the following page you'll find an example of my to-do list (usually a long list of daily grinds—the minutiae of life) versus my priority list (very focused and prioritized).

MY TO-DO LIST	MY PRIORITY LIST
• Weight-train 30 minutes • Run 6 km • Take Cooper for a walk • Cook red-lentil & coconut soup • Make dinner (stir-fry mushrooms, roasted potatoes, baked cauliflower, tofu and peppers) • Answer student emails • Mark student papers • Pick up dry-cleaning • Clear winter mess out of garage • Pick up groceries • Get mail • Take Cooper for vaccinations • Prepare PowerPoint for next lecture • Do laundry • Drink more water • Book salon appointment • Call cell phone company to discuss latest bill	• Time-block 3 hours to write next chapter of book. • Write out a few media sound bites for press kit.

Time-Blocking

Extraordinary results don't just happen. YOU have to make them happen. So, ignore the chaos and the noise of your daily life by blocking out three hours every day to work on your priority goals.

Time-blocking is essential for productivity. We are bombarded by hundreds of distractions every day. You must filter out the nonsense ALL the time or you'll spend your days reacting to frivolous issues instead of being proactive with your dreams. Not everything is urgent. Things, people, issues . . . they can wait until you've completed your TIME BLOCK.

Each hour, whether it's taken on its own or consecutively, must NOT be interrupted. Shut off all technology and make sure you can't be reached for that time period. If you do NOT control your time you will NOT control your results.[13]

Here's an example of my own time block:

Monday to Friday: 9:30 a.m.–noon and 12:45 p.m.–2:45 p.m.

Saturday and Sunday: Noon–3:00 p.m.

When is your time block? Remember, nothing should be allowed to interrupt that three-hour block of time.

TIPS

- *When do you feel most productive?* Figure out if you're a morning person or a night owl. (Hint: that's when you need to be working on your most important goals.)
- *Establish a routine.* Get up at the same time every day; go to bed at the same time; eat the same breakfast; pick your outfits for the week on Sunday, and so on. The more routines you have, the more effective you'll be because you'll be saving time.
- *Pick a system that works for you.* My time scheduling system may not work for you, and that's O.K. But you NEED a system. Otherwise you'll be reacting to situations.

Here's an example of my daily schedule. This is a typical day for me.	
5:00 a.m.	Wake up!
5:15–6:00 a.m.	Exercise, either a run (5–8km) or weights (30 min. program. I'm now doing Beach Body's 21Day Fix).
6:00–6:30 a.m.	Shower, change and make breakfast (either a bowl of oatmeal with cinnamon and fruits or a vegan protein shake). Ryo wakes up; Steve changes her and brings her downstairs for play time.
6:30–7:00 a.m.	Unload dishwasher and get Ryo's breakfast ready. Load dishwasher with breakfast dishes and wipe down kitchen. Feed Cooper breakfast and give him fresh water.
7:00–8:30 a.m.	Play with Ryo. Make sure she's dressed for preschool, brush her hair and teeth, put moisturizer or SPF on her face (she hates this, this will be a battle.)
8:30–9:00 a.m.	Drive Ryo to daycare and drive back home.
9:00–9:30 a.m.	Walk Cooper.
9:30 a.m.–noon	**TIME BLOCK: Work (writing blog postings, editing book, working on my lectures, cold-calling potential clients).**
Noon–12:30 p.m.	Feed Cooper and eat lunch while watching YouTube clips of comedians or viral late-night talk-show clips.
12:30–12:45 p.m.	Do a load of laundry or cook.
12:45–2:45 p.m.	**TIME BLOCK: Work (same as before).**
2:45–3:00 p.m.	One of following— dishes, another load of laundry, cook or clean up Ryo's playroom.
3:00–3:20 p.m.	Walk Cooper for 20 minutes.
3:20–3:30 p.m.	Put laundry away. Wash Cooper's bed mats.
3:30–5:30 p.m.	**TIME BLOCK: Work (same as before).**
5:30–6:00 p.m.	Feed Cooper dinner, then pick up Ryo at daycare and drive home.
6:00–8:00 p.m.	Family time with Ryo. Eat dinner, play, bathtime, read stories in bed from 7:30 to 8:00 p.m.
8:00–8:30 p.m.	Wind down with Steve for 30 minutes.
8:30–9:30 p.m.	**TIME BLOCK: Work (same as before).**
9:30–10:30 p.m.	Read in bed.
10:30 p.m.	Go to sleep!

By the way, when my schedule falls apart, this is what I do: I order take-out instead of cooking; I stop cleaning; I have a real partner who steps up and helps out. When I can afford it I outsource things (hiring cleaners, etc.).

Do a Performance Review

Just because you were super-productive on Tuesday doesn't mean you get to take Wednesday off. Just because you scored a new client/deal/project in the morning doesn't mean the rest of the day is a write-off.

This also works the other way around: if you had a crummy morning, that doesn't entitle you to slack off. Just because you got a crappy mark on your assignment or got reamed out by your boss doesn't mean you get the rest of the day to sulk about it.

Ask yourself: Did I live up to my fullest potential today?

The only way to keep on track with your progress is to conduct weekly performance reviews on yourself.

Ask yourself every night: *"Did I live up to my fullest potential today? On a scale from one to 10, how successful was I this week, compared to how successful I could have been?"*

There are always areas for improvement.

One of the downsides of academia is the *student mentality*, which does you no favors in the real world. The real world has managers, deadlines and projects—if you cannot complete your work *in its entirety and on time*, someone is getting fired, someone isn't getting promoted.

Do yourself a favor and start the habit of nightly/weekly performance reviews.

Scoring yourself is scary because we'd all like to think we're awesome (and awesome all day long). But we're not. We've all lost a few days on Pinterest or Instagram, lounging at Starbucks, trying to figure out how to increase the credit limit on our Visa cards, instead of working to bring in more money.

Self-analysis is the key to keeping you on track to achieving your potential and generating tremendous amounts of success.

Start correcting these problems immediately. Take action today. Not tomorrow, not on the weekend, not on Monday (the #1 day for diets).

Take action today.

Evaluate your Time

It's easy to fall behind in your work or get sidetracked by working on less important tasks (like watching Netflix or cleaning the house), when you really should be working on the more difficult things that have a bigger long-term pay-off.

TIPS

- *Evaluate yourself.* Evaluating yourself doesn't have to be complicated or time-consuming. It's as simple as adding up the number of tasks on your priority list that you actually completed.
- *Schedule your evaluation.* You must spend five minutes every night writing down your goals for the next day and evaluating yourself for today.
- *Evaluate whether the task was completed, not the quality or results of the task.*[14] You're scoring yourself ONLY on whether you did the task or not. Don't get into an internal battle with yourself as to whether or not the results were perfect. It's daily consistent progress that moves you closer and closer to your ultimate dream for yourself and your career.
- *Aim for progress, not perfection.* Do NOT expect to complete 100% of your daily goals. This is unrealistic and sets you up for disappointment. Always aim for 100% but be happy if you get to 80%. What you want is to be progressively better each day, each week.
- *Analyze what your score means.* If you're consistently failing to complete certain tasks, you may be purposely avoiding them or maybe you're back in that perfectionism mindset. Maybe you're avoiding the more difficult tasks because you're so scared of failing that you don't even bother trying.

- *Align your daily goals with your long-term vision for yourself.* What does success look like for you? What does fulfilling your potential mean for you? Write down your long-term vision or plan for your life and make sure that your daily goals align with it. —I know I'm repeating myself, but this is such an integral step for success.

- *Recognize the time traps.* Where are you wasting time? Is it reading your emails first thing in the morning? Are you completing tasks that are super-easy and require no real effort in the morning when you're fresh and energetic? Are you wasting time driving in traffic and listening to the radio instead of audio CD's that will motivate you? Are you wasting time running errands (I used to do this!), instead of saving all your errands for one day of the week? Everyone is different, but we all know where we waste our time. Be honest with yourself.

Nobody can work on their dreams all day long. We all need to pay the bills. The most effective way I can work my day-job and pursue my dreams is to do *split shifts.* I work a few hours, then it's housework/childcare/food prep/dog care, then back to work. But I always do the most important work at the beginning of the day.

You'll find a time productivity template on the next page. Use it to assess your progress toward your daily goals. Remember, your list of goals should NOT be an endless. Keep focused on the one or two things that will make a substantial difference in getting you closer to fulfilling your potential. You need very specific goals in each of your key areas (career, fitness, personal) to keep you on track.

If you want to control your results (the only thing that matters!), you must control your time. You must completely and utterly dominate time. You *own* time. You don't work for time, time works for you. Get it?

Productivity Template

Vision statement:

Today's Priority List: Time Block:

1. ....

2. ....

3. ....

Score yourself: .... /3

What am I grateful for?

....

List your successes today: ....
....

Top time wasters or struggles today:

....

Strategy to overcome your struggle(s):

....

Don't Call Me On the Phone!

Are you on fire? Are you stranded on the highway? Are you being attacked? If not, why are you calling me on the phone? We need to stop this, people.

Stop wasting people's time. Time is a commodity that we need to manage. Hell, we need to dominate time. It's not something that is endlessly expendable.

Stop allowing people to waste your time. Stop accepting phone calls from people you know will steal 30, 60 or even 90+ minutes from you. You can't be the "go-to" person for all your friends' problems.

I'm not saying you should be a jerk and never talk on the phone. But you need to put up some boundaries. Most importantly, you need to differentiate between *needing* to talk to someone and *wanting* to talk to someone.

Gone are the days of endlessly gabbing on the phone. One of my best friends from high school and I were just laughing about this. Who has time to talk on the phone anymore? So we worked out a better plan to stay connected. How about 10-minute bursts? You don't have to literally time yourself, but I'd rather catch up with the people that matter to me in short little bursts than wait weeks on end to talk to them for an extended period of time because our lives are so busy.

We allow people to waste our time because we've internalized the people-pleasing gene. We don't want to hurt people's feelings and if someone is in a difficult situation, we think it's our duty and responsibility as nurturers to help them out.

We also allow people to waste our time because we'll do anything to avoid conflict. Wow, do women hate confrontation. It's worth repeating. We'll do ANYTHING to avoid confrontation.

I've known women who've been talked into baking wedding cakes (FOR FREE) and they're not even bakers; women who've offered to dog-sit for weeks on end without compensation;

women who've proofread and edited someone's work only to see that favor not reciprocated. These women could not stop saying "Yes." (That's another chapter!)

TIPS

- *Use a courteous, professional-sounding statement* the next time you need to cut a conversation short. For instance: *"I'd love to hear more about this, but unfortunately now is not a good time for me. Perhaps we can discuss at a later date. I hope everything works out well."* (NOTE: This is obviously not to be used for people on the brink of a major personal catastrophe).
- *Prepare to be interrogated.* People will want to know why you're saying "no." They'll guilt you into helping with, talking about, or listening to their problems. You don't need to provide excuses or justify why you're not available. Remember: Are they on fire? Is it an emergency? If not, you know what to do now.

What will you say to someone the next time you need to say "no"?

What Will You Sacrifice?

Right now, figure out what you need to give up in order to take your career to the next level. What can you do, what can you change? What modifications can you make in your schedule to maximize your time?

For me, it's giving up a 6 a.m. start to the day. Bye-bye, 6 a.m.—you were so good to me. Now it's 5 a.m. And losing that hour is sometimes brutal. But it allows me to go for a run, shower and change by the time my daughter gets up at 6:30 a.m.

Another thing I do now is *work through lunch.* No more 30- or (gasp!) 45-minute lunch breaks. Nope. As Fredrik Ecklund from *Million Dollar Listing New York* says, "Lunch is a big waste of time, so I generally work right through it."[15]

I also *do all my errands on one day.* This is challenging, but I've had to tweak my schedule so I'm not wasting time going to the grocery store or hairdresser on different days. Now everything gets done on the same day (most of the time). OK, I'm still working on this.

Most importantly, I've *stopped procrastinating.* I've stopped wishing my life was different and started taking impressive levels of action. I've stopped self-medicating through shopping, ice cream and exercise. (Have you tried Coconut Bliss ice cream?? Oh my . . . the Cappuccino flavor is SO good. OK, I digress!) I've realized that purchasing a product (why do I own so many lipsticks?!) is a momentary release, but the work still awaits me when I get home.

Resistance.
Procrastination.
Denial.
Unhappiness.
Stress.
Anxiety.
I've realized that all I have to do . . . **is the work.**

I delay gratification.

I have a choice.

Every single day, I can choose the more difficult task (writing, cold-calling, selling, self-promotion), or I can procrastinate, delay, avoid, resist (and waste my time cleaning, cooking, running errands, shopping, and over-thinking EVERY. SINGLE. THING).

That's my story.

What's yours?

Delaying Gratification

We live in a world obsessed with instant gratification. We want it all and we want it now.

Ever have to wait a full five minutes for your Starbucks Frappuccino? You texted three people to complain about the wait during those five minutes, right? Or you rolled your eyes, tapped your fingernails on the counter or sighed really loudly.

People lose their minds because they have to wait for something.

Good things require excessive amounts of work and effort, time and dedication. Nothing good comes immediately. We've forgotten the value of long-term goals.

You're only as good as your last day.

Do you know that our attention span has declined to eight seconds?[16] The average person doesn't read entire articles anymore, she just scans headlines. That's why so many people have an incomplete understanding of vital issues that affect their lives.

Shorter attention spans are caused by the barrage of external stimulation we're under. You need to be very selective in what you're exposing yourself to so that you always remain on task, on schedule and working toward your dream, not someone else's.

Short attention spans equal an inability to see the bigger picture. They lead to impatience and even poor reading skills.

Persistence is key! What you do today and tomorrow and the next month matters. You may not see the benefit for a while, but that doesn't mean you should stop.

Keep working, keeping putting in unimaginable amounts of effort. It will pay off, because most people are not able or willing to keep up the pace for extended periods of time. You'll smoke the competition, if you just keep your long-term vision in sight. You'll be achieving success, while others are checking their email for the thirtieth time that day, or posting mindless updates on Facebook.

Remember, it's all about delaying immediate gratification (for example: checking your phone . . . again), in order to remain on task and keep working on that long-term vision.

THE MARSHMALLOW EFFECT

Psychologists tested the willpower of toddlers by offering them either one marshmallow now, or two at a later point. They followed up with the same toddlers years later and found that those who had delayed the immediate gratification of eating one marshmallow had higher SAT scores and lower levels of substance abuse. Their parents rated them as handling stress better, being better organized, and as having enhanced concentration skills. Learning to delay gratification is a critical tool for lifelong success.[17] The good news is that self-control is a skill that can be learned, by practicing delaying gratification.

How do I delay gratification? By not purchasing something for myself (clothing, shoes, a $6 latté) until I've achieved my task for the day. For example, I gave myself a deadline to finish this book. Once I completed the entire first draft I bought myself a new outfit! I always treat myself AFTER I've completed the most important goal. For instance, after I make 50 cold calls looking for companies I can give talks to, I'll head over to the bookstore to browse the aisles and buy a new book.

I had to GIVE UP certain things in order to make my dream of living off my writing and public talks a reality. Most importantly, I gave up the security of having the regular paycheck with benefits, including health insurance, that I had when I was working in the university system. I gave up eating out and having an entertainment budget. I gave up vacations, movies and so much more.

If I want to be an entrepreneur, risk is inevitable. BUT the eventual payoff will be extraordinary. So, in short, I had to learn to delay gratification in the immediate moment so that in the future I could have ultimate gratification, including financial freedom and security, all while being my own boss.

Barrier #2

Procrastination and Perfectionism

Some failure in life is inevitable. It is impossible to live without failing at something, unless you live so cautiously that you might as well not have lived at all—in which case you fail by default.

—J.K. Rowling, author

Good, now you have your schedule on track and time is working for you, but the negative voice inside your head is still nagging at you and you've said yes to everyone and everything but you and your career. Now what?

Procrastination

No good paper was ever written the day an assignment was due. A+ papers aren't written during an all-nighter the night before when you're buzzed from Red Bull and donuts. Believe me, I've read those papers. And I've also been that student starting a paper at 11:00 p.m. when it's due at eight the next morning.

Handing in late papers seems to be a rite-of-passage for undergraduate (and graduate!) students. I've been there. I was a procrastinator, too. And eventually I had to stop. I remember the exact night. I was staying up, working on a sociology paper and silently cursing myself for doing this yet again. I was stressed, in tears, completely anxious, and I didn't have a clue what I was writing about. I started at the last minute and tried writing a phenomenal paper, and as the hours ticked by, I began lowering my expectations of the grade. *"Oh, this is going to be an A paper for SURE. . . . OK, I'd be happy with a 76. . . . Oh, whatever, as long as I get at least a 60 I'll be fine. . . . Shit, I hope I pass. . . . God, this is awful, it's embarrassingly bad. I definitely failed."*

See what I mean? Lowering your goals and expectations is never a good plan.

When you're organized you don't react to situations, you are proactive.

When you procrastinate you can bet on your printer failing you at 3 a.m. You can bet that your USB will be infected with some virus, rendering all your work useless so you have to start over again. When you're stressed and late and procrastinating, the worst-case scenario will always happen.

—Because printer problems and toner problems and Word formatting problems and USB problems don't bother an organized person. Sure, they're annoying, but these little blips do not *destroy* organized people, they don't *ruin* their days or cause undue anxiety, because there's TIME. There's time left over to fix these issues and still meet the deadline.

I made this mistake as a new mother. I expected to be able to do my work on certain days and when my daughter was sick or just needed more of my attention, my schedule went out the window. If I left preparing my lecture to the last minute, I was stressed! It taught me to NEVER expect I'd have time tomorrow to do something that I should have completed today.

Organized people always leave room for the unexpected. Because that's just life, and something always comes up. For instance, I've learned that Ryo (as a typical 3-year-old) doesn't really like to be rushed in the mornings. So I have to start trying to get her ready 15 minutes earlier in order to avoid a toddler meltdown and me throwing her shoes across the room in frustration. True story! I was actually so overwhelmed one day that I threw one shoe across the room, then calmly walked back and got the other shoe to throw. I texted my girlfriend immediately afterwards and she replied, "As long as you didn't throw Ryo across the room, you're good."

Stop Dreaming. Start Working!

Were you born to be an actor? A writer? A lawyer? Professor, artist, dancer or architect? Who knows? But the only way to find out is through action.

What action are you taking *right now, today* to discover your potential? Creative people create. Athletes train. Writers write. They all act because they know no other way of being.

Get out of your head; get out of your way. Take action.

Stop thinking about it.

Doing the work every single day is the only thing that matters.

Working on your potential every day allows your ego to dissolve, forces the negative voice in your mind to dissipate, and fosters creativity. The more time you devote to your craft, the more bulletproof you are to criticisms, haters, and your own internal procrastination tendencies.

Dreaming won't win you the lottery. Taking action is what matters.

Want inspiration? Watch Beyoncé performing "Run the World" from the 2011 Billboard Music Awards. No amount of daydreaming created this performance. It was pure dedication, hundreds of hours of training and commitment. You can't fake that kind of precision and immaculate choreography.

She took action. She worked for it. The results speak for themselves: one of my all-time favorite musical performances.

The Myths of Perfectionism

Sad but true story: I once knew a fellow graduate student in the history Ph.D. program. A classic Type-A over-achieving perfectionist (I recognized myself in her). She failed for the first time in graduate school and really struggled with her courses and developing her dissertation topic. She stumbled and was so horrified at her mistakes she DROPPED OUT of school. Within a year, she was back living with her parents. Five years later, she was working part-time at the bookstore. She went from a full scholarship in a Ph.D. program at an Ivy League school to making $15 an hour, all because she couldn't handle not being perfect.

Perfectionism is not about wanting to do your best. Perfectionism isn't about self-improvement, personal growth or progress. No, perfectionism will harm you; it is destructive and addictive.

Perfectionism impedes your ability to achieve success, because you're never fully, completely and utterly invested in what you're doing or creating when you're a perfectionist. Perfectionism prevents you from taking a risk and going ALL IN because at the root of perfectionism is fear. Fear that you're making a mistake or that you'll fail at something. Fear that you won't live up to other people's expectations. Fear that you won't achieve what you really want to achieve.

Researcher Brené Brown has coined the term *life paralysis*.[18] These are opportunities and experiences you miss because you're so busy trying to be perfect that you never try something unless you're absolutely certain you'll succeed.

How often have you avoided something because you knew you weren't going to be perfect at it?

We're so scared of failure, of making mistakes, of disappointing others (and ourselves) that we don't try new things, we don't take risks, and we don't go beyond our comfort zones and push through the boundaries.

Perfectionism is an unrealistic and unattainable goal. Nothing and no one is perfect (look at how many times the iPhone has been revised or updated!). Perfection is never attained. According to Brown:[19]

- Perfectionism is destructive. Full stop. Perfectionism hurts you.
- Perfectionism is delusional, because we want to be "perceived" by others as perfect. We cannot control nor manage other people's expectations or feelings about us. We can only control our own actions and our responses to others. That's it.
- The quest for perfectionism never succeeds and all the emotions and judgments we were hoping to avoid (shame, ridicule, blame, rejection and fear) never go away; they creep into our lives whether we like it or not.

So how do you overcome perfectionism?

- Develop an awareness of your perfectionist tendencies. Perfectionism exists on a continuum and some people's perfectionism creeps up only under certain circumstances or around certain people. Figure out your trigger points.
- Acknowledge your vulnerabilities, your fears and anxieties. Realize we all have our own individual fears and that you're never alone on this journey.
- Realize that sometimes "done" is better than perfect.

Aim for Completion, Not Perfection

One of my students' main stumbling blocks has been their desire for perfection. This perfectionist quest leads to procrastination, all-nighters, unbelievable amounts of anxiety, and then failure to complete the task at hand. They never finish the project, or hand it in late.

In the real world there are no "late assignments." There are no "seven-day extensions" to help you through.

You must aim for completion, not perfection. Perfection is paralysis.

When I was completing my Ph.D., I suffered from this same disease. I wanted things to be perfect. I wanted my research question to be PERFECT. —Until finally someone told me that my Ph.D. was not the end of my journey, but just a stepping stone to the rest of my life's work. That was a total "a-ha!" moment. So I channeled my inner Oprah and got to work!

I realized I didn't need to solve every woman's health issue. I didn't need to figure out all the problems with the food industry. I just needed to complete the degree. Then get started on the rest of my life.

I aim to do my best work at all times. And when my best isn't enough, I realize there's another option: I need to JUST GET IT DONE.

I can work hours upon hours on my lectures, trying to create the perfect balance of pop-culture references and short, funny video clips interspersed with relevant sociological material that will keep my students off their phones during the lecture. Sometimes it comes together beautifully, and other times it doesn't. But I show up every week and give my lecture regardless. I don't phone it in. I don't call in sick. And I stopped pulling all-nighters.

Leaving things to the last minute, arriving late, or pulling all-nighters are signs that:

- You're not that organized;
- You have way too much to handle;
- You haven't prioritized what matters most; and
- You're probably spending too much time on low-pay- off short-term goals, rather than aligning your daily priority list with your long-term vision.

But I didn't figure that out until well after my undergraduate days.

While completing my Ph.D., I had a sign above my desk that read: "Aim for completion, not perfection, and just GET IT DONE."

Whatever it is: Just. Get. It. Done.

Here Come the Excuses

Have you ever uttered the words "*Yeah,* I wish I could do that, *BUT—*" or "*Yeah,* I should have done that, *BUT—*" or "*Yeah,* I always wanted to do that, *BUT—*"?

These are excuses you give yourself for why you didn't do something. You're just lying to yourself—no one else.

Could have. Would have. Should have.

BUT. You. Didn't. That's the truth.

Everyone is a star athlete in their own minds. Everyone is a writer. Everyone is articulate and eloquent and persuasive. The difference with the successful athlete, writer or salesperson is that they practiced, they trained, they prepared and, most importantly, *they took action.* Everyone else just thinks about success, daydreams about success, talks about success, but never acts upon it.

Start taking action today on what will move you forward in your career, education and life goals. Do not wait for tomorrow. Come up with ONE THING you can do today to move your life forward. Pick the most difficult task because you'll feel like a total superstar when you complete it.

This is where most people get lost. They live in their minds and never come down to reality (graduate students, I'm talking to you here!). Creating success isn't about luck. It's about hard work. Successful people didn't luck out. They worked for it, planned for it and then took action every single day.

TIPS

- *Take action.* What type of action are you taking to move you forward? Just a little bit? A fair amount? Or MASSIVE action?[20] Are you taking extraordinary, impressive and outstanding amounts of action? Because that's the only kind that counts.

- *Evaluate yourself every day.* How productive were you today? What results did you produce? It's not about effort, it's about results. This fact messes people up. My students, for example, think they deserve an A+ if they worked really hard. But it's not about your effort or your intentions. It's about the results. It's challenging to objectively evaluate yourself. We may think we're doing well, but when you actually see your progress written down, you'll probably decide you need to increase your efforts.

- *Stop underestimating how much work, effort and persistence are required for success.* People think they can send out a few tweets, write a few blogs and people will flock to their site. NO! I can't emphasize this enough. Recognize that anything worth having takes enormous amounts of dedication. Be willing to do what others are not. Be willing to call 100 clients to promote your services, while most people will only call 10. Be willing to send out 100 emails looking for a new job. Be willing to visit 100 businesses in person, because no one else will.

Start viewing success as your only option. There is no Plan B. There is no lottery. There is only the reality you create for yourself. Success is your responsibility. Own it.

Resistance

What excuses do you use for not achieving success? What lies do you tell yourself about why you haven't achieved greatness?

We often attribute our failure to achieve success to external forces. It's our lack of money, time or resources. We blame our spouses, partners, children and friends. But more often than not, failure is attributable to what Steven Pressfield in his brilliant book *War of Art* calls resistance.

Resistance is basically procrastination. You're resisting what you need to do.

You need to stop doing the important things SOME of the time, and start working on the important things ALL OF THE TIME.

As Pressfield says: "Resistance is not a peripheral opponent. Resistance arises from within. It is self-generated and self-perpetuated. Resistance is the enemy within."[21]

I was supposed to start cold-calling for my business, to generate interest in my talks and workshops and my upcoming book. But I haven't made any cold calls.

My house is being renovated and the place is messy and disorganized with painters and builders all over. So I lie to myself and pretend that no one could work in such anti-feng shui conditions. I actually convince myself that no creativity could transpire among the beige walls and dusty floors. . . . That's resistance. It's not the painters or the contractors in my house that are preventing me from succeeding in my business.

The hurdles lie within. The lies I tell myself are insidious because time is what they feed on, and time is what I keep friggin' feeding them. Time to over-think, time to ruminate. Time to reflect when I should be taking action.

"Resistance will tell you anything to keep you from doing your work. It will perjure, fabricate, falsify; seduce, bully, cajole. Resistance is protean. It will assume any form, if that's what it takes to deceive you. IT will reason with you like a lawyer or jam a nine-millimeter in your face

like a stickup man. Resistance has no conscience. IT will pledge anything to get a deal, then double-cross you as soon as your back is turned. IF you take Resistance at its word, you deserve everything you get. Resistance is always lying and always full of shit."[22]

What lies do you tell yourself?

THE CYCLE OF PROCRASTINATION AND PERFECTIONISM

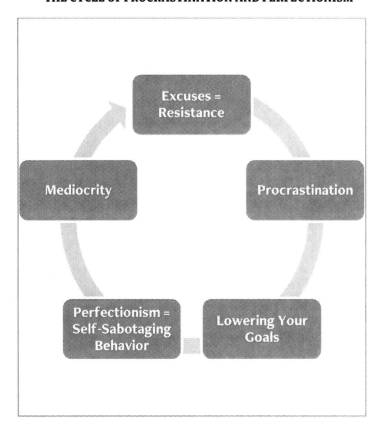

What is Self-Compassion?

As women we're SO hard on ourselves all the time. We ridicule ourselves for failing at a task, when we should be pumping ourselves up. We call ourselves names and endlessly berate ourselves for our mistakes, instead of figuring out why we messed up and how we can move on.

At the root of these nagging negative voices is our lack of self-compassion. *Well, what the heck is self-compassion and why is it important for success?*

According to Dr. Kristin Neff, self-compassion has three elements:[23]

1. SELF-KINDNESS. "Self-compassion entails being warm and understanding toward ourselves when we suffer, fail, or feel inadequate, rather than ignoring our pain or flagellating ourselves with self-criticism."

2. COMMON HUMANITY. "Frustration at not having things exactly as we want is often accompanied by an irrational but pervasive sense of isolation—as if 'I' were the only person suffering or making mistakes."

3. MINDFULNESS. "Self-compassion also requires taking a balanced approach to our negative emotions so that feelings are neither suppressed nor exaggerated. This equilibrated stance stems from the process of relating personal experiences to those of others who are also suffering, thus putting our own situation into a larger perspective."

Successful people tend to possess greater levels of self-compassion. They treat themselves better. They don't dwell on their mistakes. They don't allow their mistakes to cloud their judgment. Successful people can analyze their failures without wallowing in agony and self-doubt.

For more information on mindfulness and self-compassion check out Dr. Neff's website: www.self-compassion.org.

Are You a People-Pleaser?

People pleasers are SO nice. Aren't they? They never say "no." They'll be there whenever and wherever you need help.

The problem is that people pleasers never help themselves. They're so overcommitted and addicted to saying "yes" that their to-do list NEVER ends. This creates a cycle of anxiety, stress, depression (emotional eating!) and resentment.

People pleasers are so worried about being perceived as selfish, rude or uncaring that they'll always put others first.

People pleasing begins with:

- *Fear of rejection.* If I say no to someone, I could lose their friendship . . . strain the relationship . . . they won't like me anymore. Then I'll have no one.
- *Fear of failure.* If I mess up people will judge, ridicule or mock me. They'll think I'm an idiot, and I'll disappoint others.
- *Lack of confidence.* You *internalize* your mistakes (I'm an idiot, I'm not good enough), and you *externalize* your successes (I couldn't have done it without the team).

The negative consequences of being a people pleaser include:

- Neglecting yourself!
- Passive-aggressively RESENTING others for demanding so much of you.
- Compromising your mental, emotional, spiritual and physical health.

The People-Pleaser Quiz

Answer "yes" or "no" to the following questions. The more "yes's" you have, the more likely it is that you're a people pleaser. Not to worry—there's a 10-step program for that!

1.	When I receive an incorrect order at Starbucks or a restaurant, I never return it. I never confront the server about it. And I usually still give a tip.	Y	N
2.	I have a bunch of bridesmaid's dresses in my closet. Even though I couldn't afford to be one, I couldn't say "no." I've been to a destination wedding . . . on my Visa card.	Y	N
3.	My to-do list has never, ever, been completed. It's three pages long.	Y	N
4.	I feel like a doormat when I say "yes." I always feel manipulated or used by others.	Y	N
5.	I can't remember the last time I said "no" to someone. I'm addicted to helping others.	Y	N
6.	Saying "yes" all the time leaves me with no time for myself, my career, and my own work.	Y	N
7.	I'm always worried about hurting other people's feelings. I'm worried they won't like me.	Y	N
8.	I'm always concerned about how others perceive me. I don't want to be perceived as rude, careless, ego-centric, unhelpful, or ungrateful.	Y	N
9.	I'm always trying to be perfect.	Y	N
10.	I allow others to change my mind in order to appear agreeable or to avoid conflict.	Y	N
11.	I'm always worrying and stressing out. I have anxiety about what others are saying about me.	Y	N
12.	I avoid confrontation and conflict at all costs.	Y	N
13.	I avoid discussing my feelings and keep them bottled up.	Y	N
14.	I always feel guilty for saying "no."	Y	N
15.	I'm constantly apologizing. All. The. Time.	Y	N
16.	I never stand up for myself.	Y	N

17.	I don't like criticism. I don't handle constructive feedback well.	Y	N
18.	I do everything myself; I rarely delegate to others.	Y	N
19.	The more I help others out, the more I think they'll like me.	Y	N
20.	I'm way more critical of myself than of others.	Y	N
21.	It's very important to be liked by others.	Y	N
22.	I hardly ever ask for help. It makes me uncomfortable to ask others to help me.	Y	N

IF you're a people pleaser, you most likely answered "yes" to the majority of these questions.

Read on, people pleasers. Let's kick this habit together!

How to Stop
Being a People-Pleaser

You can stop putting other people's needs ahead of your own. You can say "no" to people and not lose their friendship. You can say "no" to your boss and not get fired. You can say "no" to your children or partner and not let guilt envelop you.

Follow these tips to stop being a people-pleaser and get your life back. Put yourself and your career FIRST.

TIPS

- *Realize you always have a choice.* Do not feel cornered.
- *Never say "yes" on the spot.* Don't get intimidated or pushed into giving a decision right away. Always think about it.
- *Practice saying "no."* Seriously, look in the mirror and say "no." *"No, I can't help you with that." "No, I'm really busy and I have no time."*
- *Do not provide a list of reasons why you're saying "no."* You do NOT need to justify your response. You're saying "no," and that's all there is to it.
- *Learn to put up boundaries.* Being assertive with your boundaries does NOT make you a bitch. It doesn't make you self-centered or egocentric. You need boundaries or there will be nothing left of you.[24]
- *Before you say "yes" to something, ask yourself four questions:* (1) Do I realistically have the time to do this? (2) Do I really want to do this? (3) What will I get out of this; how will I benefit? (4) What will this cost me? —If you'll resent the time spent helping someone else out, don't do it. If helping someone out is going to set you back in your own work, don't do it. If you actually have little desire or inclination to help out, don't do it. If saying "yes" will cost you in some way (more than you're getting back), then just say "no." If you're

going to expend time, energy, and money that you just can't afford to give, please just say "no."

- *Consider setting a time frame.* You'll only help someone out from 8 a.m. to 9 a.m. You will help out for 45 minutes and then you have to go. BUT if you anticipate that one hour will easily turn into two hours, then STOP. Don't do it. Don't say yes. It's sort of like potato chips: If you can't just eat a few chips, then don't buy the bag. If you can't help out for a limited amount of time, you need to walk away.

- *Assess what you've done for yourself and your career every day.* Have you spent more time working on someone else's dreams than your own? Have you spent more time fixing, solving or listening to other people's problems than working on your career, than working on fulfilling your potential? Then it's time to change.

- *Take care of yourself.* What have you done today for your own mind, body and spirit? —For example, exercise, yoga, meditation, journaling, art work. What gives you joy? Make sure you do that every day, even if it's for just 15 minutes.

- *Realize you'll never please everyone.* There will always be haters, there will always be people who want more and more and more from you. In every class I teach I have students who think I'm the BEST professor they've ever had, alongside students who want to slash my tires. This will never change. So don't waste your energies trying to get everyone to love you. It'll never happen.

Barrier #3

Fear

I'm scared all the time. You have to have fear in order to have courage. I'm a courageous person because I'm a scared person

—*Ronda Rousey,*
Olympic medalist and UFC
champion

From UFC fighters to politicians to moms sending kids out into the world, we all experience fear, and it can stop us in our tracks. This is something you can change.

What Are You So Afraid Of?

So many of us live our lives in fear of something. What are you so afraid of? Check all that apply.

- ☐ Fear of failure
- ☐ Fear of not being liked
- ☐ Fear of being judged
- ☐ Fear of being ridiculed, mocked or laughed at
- ☐ Fear of looking stupid (or sounding stupid)
- ☐ Fear of parental disapproval
- ☐ Fear that you won't make any money doing this
- ☐ Fear of making the wrong decision
- ☐ Fear of making a fool of yourself
- ☐ Fear of someone stealing your ideas
- ☐ Fear that everyone is looking at you
- ☐ Fear of your relationship ending
- ☐ Fear of someone saying "I told you so"
- ☐ Fear that you have no talent or creativity
- ☐ Fear that you don't have enough education, skills or experience
- ☐ Fear that you're too old to try this
- ☐ Fear that you're not pretty enough/thin enough/cool enough
- ☐ Fear that you don't have the right space or environment to work in

When my students meet with me in my office, I usually ask them why they don't speak up in class or why this is the first time we've met—and their answers are usually the following: *"I was scared. You intimidate me. I've never spoken to a professor before. I didn't know how to ask for help. I thought I would look like an idiot for asking this in class. I've been procrastinating."*

It's all based in fear.

I have colleagues who've wanted to write a book for 10 years (!) and never started.

I've also known people who've written numerous articles but were too scared to send them off for review or publication.

I've had students in their final year of university tell me that I'm the first and only professor they've ever spoken to throughout their entire university career! —This is shocking (and so sad) to me. More importantly, this needs to stop.

As women, we need to stop taking things so personally, stop obsessing with the idea that everyone is thinking about us (they're not). You must assume the best of others, not the worst.

Professors don't wake up each day eager to destroy students. Your boss doesn't start each day with a voodoo doll ritual. No one is out to "get you."

Fear will mess with your mind, it will create doubt about your abilities, it will cause you to downplay your accomplishments and, worse of all, it will create a vicious cycle in which you consistently underestimate yourself. Eventually you stop reaching for things, and then you're exactly where you feared you'd be: *nowhere.*

Take this ALL IN challenge:

Do one thing that pushes you out of your damn comfort zone. Something that makes you feel completely uncomfortable. For some of my students it's as simple as talking to a stranger. For others it's speaking aloud in a meeting. But you must speak up. Voice your opinions. Let others know you exist.

Let me know how it works out. Send me an email, tweet me. I'll respond.

By the way: writing a blog and posting YouTube videos scares me. Putting my words out there for anyone to dissect or, worse, to criticize (gasp!) is scary. But the alternative (not going ALL IN to my career) is so, so much worse than the fear of public ridicule or failure.

Regret is forever. Criticism is momentarily hurtful. But you grow from criticism and then you move the hell onward.

Fear Is Holding You Back

Fear is holding you back.

Fear will destroy your life. Fear will prevent you from achieving your full potential and force you into a life of mediocrity. Fear will make you that person who silently wishes for a better life but never acts upon that wish. Years from now, you'll look back and wish your life had been different. But you allowed fear to control your decisions and now, where are you?

I see it every day in the classroom. My female students are petrified of speaking up and they let fear dictate the course of their lives.

That's one of the inspirations for creating my blog, social club and this book: I want to get women to push through their fears.

For every female student who keeps her hand down in class, doesn't speak up, doesn't ask questions, and doesn't engage with the material or environment she's in, you can bet there are dozens of others (usually men) who are rushing full force to take advantage of every opportunity to have their voices heard (even when they have nothing to say).

> **Everyone is fearful; the difference is in how you manage your fears.**

Successful people turn their fears into motivators, while unsuccessful people just complain about them.

Oh, and by the way, why do you think you're the only one who's fearful?

Fear is a sign that you're stretching yourself out of your comfort zone. —That's a good thing, because it'll take you further away from being average, mediocre and part of the status quo.

No fear means you're not putting enough effort toward achieving your dreams.

Harnessing your fears so they work for you means:

- Realizing you'll never have it all perfectly figured out.
- Accepting that your life will be messy at times. Learn to love the mess. (Your career will move laterally, then horizontally, then on a little bit of a roller coaster; your house might be unkempt, you may not exercise every day, the dishes are

dirty, the dog is crapping in the backyard—messiness, see what I mean?)

- Waiting until you're absolutely prepared to do something means you'll NEVER DO ANYTHING. Stop waiting and start acting.

Get rid of those antiquated ideas that women aren't supposed to be opinionated, outspoken or aggressive. If I'm not aggressive with my career and getting the things I want in life, who will be aggressive for me? Who will fight for me? No one will. That's the truth.

Stop waiting for permission to do something new or different. Let's start using our fears to our advantage and go ALL IN. We can make a difference.

Take a Risk Already!

Do you know that men will apply for a job if they have 60% of the qualifications needed, while women will apply only if they have 100%?! Isn't that crazy? Yet I've made this mistake myself numerous times, and so have my female colleagues.[25]

We talk ourselves OUT of taking a risk, such as applying for a job or promotion, because the negative voice in our heads convinces us we aren't ready, aren't worthy, or we'll never get it anyhow, so why bother?

This mindset holds us back. More men apply for leadership roles than women; therefore, more men get leadership positions. It doesn't mean they're better suited to those jobs; they just take more risks and are willing to fail more often. WHY?

Because men do NOT internalize failure, while women do. Women ruminate. Women talk about their mistakes with every girlfriend, confidant and colleague. Women cry about it, then think about it some more. THEY. WILL. BE. CONSUMED. BY. THEIR. MISTAKES. Meanwhile, men have gone out and applied for 12 more positions while we're crying about the one we didn't get.

Ambition is expected of men, but it's more of an "option" for women. While women get called "bossy" when they're ambitious, men are congratulated and applauded for their drive and ambition.

Recently I was told my daughter (she's 3) was a little bossy at day care. I proudly nodded my head, thinking "Yes! I'm doing something right"—and then the school gave me tips on how she could share more and be "nicer" with her friends. —*WRONG THINKING.* I don't want her to grow up and learn how to share, so that she can be stuck in the middle of the pack.

I'm trying to raise a leader here, and if you want to call her ambition "bossiness," that's on you.

I'm raising a champion. So, when my daughter sees a job posting and she's only got 50% of the qualifications, she'll apply because it's ingrained in her that she's worthy of being a leader, she's smart enough, she knows enough, and she's got just the right amount of fear to push her through.

TIPS

- *Start small.* Reach out of your comfort zone frequently with low-pain drills. Talk in front of five people first, and then start speaking out in meetings or larger classrooms. Put yourself out there.
- *Do something every day that scares you.* Seriously. Apply for a job that you think is totally out of your league. The job requires French? You can't speak French? Apply for the job.
- *Invest in yourself.* Successful people invest in what they need to succeed—a book, a seminar, a headhunter, a writing clinic, a public speaking workshop. Unsuccessful people just complain about the cost.
- *READ.* According to the Pew Research Center, the average North American reads one book a year.[26] Nope, that's not a typo. I'm serious. Look it up. The average CEO reads *five books a month.*
- *Find supportive friends or a social group.* Lean on these people to help push you forward and call you out on your crap when you're not pushing yourself hard enough.
- *One risk is not enough.* Stop patting yourself on the back just because you stepped out of your comfort zone once, or applied for one new job, or did one full day of productive work. That may be good, but you need to be GREAT. So keep putting forth GREAT effort day after day after day. Enough is never enough.

Learn from Your Failures

If you're not failing or making mistakes, then you're not taking enough risks—you're not stretching yourself out of your comfort zone. If you limit your goals you limit your potential.

Taking a risk always means failure is an option. When you realize that, you'll stop being scared of failure and look at it as just another barrier to overcome.

Failing multiple times will get you closer to reaching your fullest potential. Believe me. No one gets to the top without failing loads of times beforehand.

Please know that fear of failure will HOLD YOU BACK from fulfilling your potential and reaching your ultimate vision for yourself.

Failures will force you to do things differently and look at problems in a new light. Failures will force you to push through your discomfort. And that's where you want to live, in the discomfort, where the butterflies in your stomach live. That means you're stretching, you're reaching, and you're moving forward.

> **If you limit your goals, you limit your potential.**

J.K. Rowling's first book, Harry Potter and the Philosopher's Stone, was rejected by 12 publishers before it was finally accepted. She was told to get a day job because the book wouldn't make any money. That book has now sold over 450 million copies.[27]

Sara Blakely, the founder of Spanx (and youngest female self-made billionaire in history), was told "no" 100 times by various manufacturers who said they couldn't produce her nylon-type undergarment, but she was determined to wear white pants with no visible panty lines.[28] Spanx now has annual sales of $250 million and analysts estimate her net worth at $1.14 billion. Who among us doesn't own a pair of Spanx?!

Arlene Dickinson was initially terrified of appearing on *Dragon's Den*, worried about how she'd look on HDTV or how she'd sound. At age 30, Arlene was a newly divorced single mother of four young children with no post- secondary education to fall back on. She's now CEO of Venture Communications, CEO of YouInc, and the author of two bestselling books[29] (they're so inspirational, read them!).[30] Arlene has a reported net worth of $80 million.[31]

Arianna Huffington's second book was rejected by publishers 36 times.[32] Two years after she lost the race for governor of California (Arnold Schwarzenegger won), she launched an Internet business. *The Huffington Post* established a viable financial model for news on the Internet; it was acquired by AOL for $315 million in 2011, making Huffington the chair, president and editor-in-chief of the Huffington Post Media Group. She is a *New York Times* best-selling author and has written 14 books. *The Huffington Post* won a Pulitzer Prize in 2012.[33]

Stephanie Meyer (of *Twilight* fame) got rejected by 14 publishers before the fifteenth accepted her manuscript. The three Twilight movies have grossed over $1.8 billion.

Vera Wang was a competitive figure skater who failed to make the Olympic team in 1968. After working for Vogue for 15 years and being passed over for the editor-in-chief position, she left the magazine to start her own company. She has a net worth of over $400 million from her numerous fashion lines.

Lady Gaga was dropped by her record label Def Jam after three months.

Katy Perry's first gospel album in 2001 was a flop, selling only 200 copies. She was dropped from the Red Hill label in 2001, dropped by Def Jam in 2003, and terminated by Columbia in 2004, but she was undeterred by these failures and completely determined to succeed. She worked back-up vocals until the success of her hit song "I Kissed a Girl" in 2006.

All of these people failed many, many times before they became hugely successful. So please, don't stop working, don't stop trying just because you failed once, twice, or ten times. Keep going! Everyone's failures are different. The key is to LEARN from these experiences and see each failure as an OPPORTUNITY for growth.

On the next page, I've provided a "non-celebrity" example by listing some of my own mistakes. Though I failed—many times!— I persevered. I kept going; I got up each time I fell down.

- It took me 10+ years to finish my undergraduate degree because I went to school part-time while working retail, trying to find "my passion."
- I went from getting A's in high school to C's and D's in my first two years of university. I had NO idea what to do with my life or what I should major in.
- I joined the debate team and the first time I debated I FROZE up and cried (in front of a room full of pre-law students).
- It took me three tries to get into a Master's program.
- Everyone said you couldn't do a research-based Master's in one year . . . but I proved them wrong.
- I found out I got rejected by the Ph.D. program in the office of the department chair. As I cried in his office, he sat there looking at me, a box of Kleenex on his desk—yet he NEVER offered to give me one measly Kleenex!—a moment I will never forget. It was a humiliating yet pivotal moment for me.
- Luckily, other universities offered me a position in their Ph.D. programs.
- I started my Ph.D. and after a year, I changed my topic, my supervisor and my committee members, because I didn't know what to do or what to study.
- Seven weeks before defending my Ph.D., I sustained a concussion and couldn't remember what my study was all about. I had to take a six-month medical leave of absence.
- During my medical leave of absence I still had to teach my courses (I needed the money), so I dimmed the lights and wore sunglasses inside because of my light sensitivity. —I was also raising a toddler, taking care of the household and on dog duty.
- I earned my Ph.D., and then switched gears out of academia to start my own business full-time.
- Everyone said it was too late to start a new business, too difficult to find a publisher for my book, too radical an idea to build a business around female empowerment and confidence issues.
- But in the end I always thought: "Why the f**k not me?"

Barrier #4
Confidence

I always believe I can beat the best, achieve the best. I always see myself in the top.

—*Serena Williams, tennis player*

Like fear, a lack of confidence is something you can overcome.

When You Hear the Word "No". . .

What does the word "no" mean for you?

Typically for women, "no" means "NO!!! You idiot, you suck! This was a stupid idea! FOREVER AND ALWAYS, NO, NO, NO, NO, NO!"

When a man hears "no," this is what he thinks: *"Oh, OK, how can I go at this another way?"* Or: *"I wonder how many 'no's' it'll take to get a 'yes.'"* Or: *"OK, let me rephrase that, let me ask in a different way."*

See the difference?

Women stop at "no." Men persist, they continue on until they hear a "yes," until they get that raise, that promotion, that new job title or that corner office.[34] In fact, men have something researchers call "honest overconfidence," causing them to "rate their performance to be 30% better than it is."[35]

Learn to enjoy the process of negotiating, so that when you hear "no," you immediately start thinking about reframing your argument to obtain a "yes." It takes skill and practice to perfect, and it gets way less scary each and every time you go ALL IN.

TIPS

- *Always, always, always ask for more.* You need to raise the asking price. Ask for more than you think you'll get. That's part of the negotiating strategy. Start low and you've got nowhere to go but down, down, down.
- *Come prepared.* When you're negotiating for something, you need to do your homework. Stick to the facts so that you don't easily get sidetracked by the rejections. Why do you deserve this promotion, raise, new responsibility, etc.? Know your value and what you bring to the organization.
- *Act like a salesperson.* My sales background was invaluable preparation for graduate school and beyond, because when you're in sales, you get used to being rejected. You get used to hearing "no," and you just have to figure out a way around it. So you must persist until you get a "yes." Ever get sold something by someone even though you had absolutely no intention of buying that day? It's an amazing experience, and

that's what you need to bring to your negotiations. I've bought makeup, jeans, shoes, jewelry, and books, because the salesperson created such a persuasive argument for why I needed those things that I just handed over my credit card. (I knew I was being sold, but I didn't mind!) That's a powerful sales presentation.

- *Do not internalize the word "no."* "No" doesn't mean you're a failure, it doesn't mean you can't handle this type of business or environment. All it means is "no" *for now*, not forever. So, stop giving the word "no" more power than it deserves.

- *Don't fear rejection. It's all just part of the game.* You must start getting comfortable with rejection (yeah, it stings BUT it also immediately helps you refocus and reframe your counter-argument). Being rejected is an instantaneous way to get feedback. OK, that didn't work...so now try this. And then keep trying again, and again, and again. Anything worth having requires multiple attempts and sustained effort. You will NOT succeed after one or two attempts.

> **I have stood on a mountain of no's for one yes.**
> —*Barbara "B" Smith, restaurateur, model, author and TV host*

So now that you know this, how many times will you try? How many times are you willing to get rejected, to fail, to hear "no," and then rise back up and try again?

Rejection

You will hear "NO" at some point in your life. You will get rejected and this will not make you feel good.

But hearing "no" doesn't mean you're incapable of getting to a "yes." It just means that at this specific moment, your product or service or idea is not ready. This doesn't mean you can't get ready, it doesn't mean you'll never succeed. ALL a rejection means is "not now" or "you haven't convinced me yet."

That's all.

Stop internalizing rejection to the point of paralysis. Stop allowing a rejection to mess with your mind and prevent you from moving forward.

I see this all the time with my girlfriends and colleagues. They didn't get hired for the job they really wanted, and they just quit. They stop completely. Instead of working through the frustration of being rejected, or being comfortable with being uncomfortable, they over-think it and let that demon of perfectionism back in.

For instance, instead of figuring out what went wrong in the interview (email and ask for feedback, any feedback at all will be useful in navigating future cover letters, or interviews), my friends internalized the notion that they suck and aren't worthy of getting a new job.

Learning how to handle constructive feedback is a tough but necessary skill that separates the winners from the losers. It separates the successful people from the day-dreamers. —Because successful people know how to USE constructive feedback, and not get used by it.

Successful people don't take criticisms personally; they leave their emotions out. Successful people figure out their mistakes based on the feedback given, and don't repeat them.

You must turn every criticism into an opportunity to improve yourself, to further develop your skills, product, services, and ideas and turn the non-believers into believers.

It may sound corny, but getting rejected and facing harsh criticism are just part of the process of achieving your ultimate vision and reaching your fullest potential.

For example, after many, many revisions of this book, I gave it to my research students to read and provide feedback. I told them to rip it to shreds. They were brutally honest (which was so refreshing) and told me I needed to cut out at least 50 to 60 pages. Ouch! They told me which parts of the book were boring or repetitive and which parts they loved. And because of their critical feedback, I did cut out 61 pages of repetitive stuff, and added in another 10 pages of specific examples and personal stories. And I can honestly say that my book is SO much better because of their critical feedback, no doubt about it. Thank you, ladies!

The next time you get rejected, take a moment to assess your reaction. Remember that it's not personal and then immediately (not tomorrow, not next week, but immediately) start crafting a better product or idea.

Get Some Self-Confidence

At any given time women vacillate between having total self-confidence and drowning in doubt and anxiety. When someone asks what you do for a living, do you keep your dreams to yourself so that you won't get criticized for not achieving them? Did someone tell you you'll never be a lawyer, doctor, graduate student, manager, public speaker, designer, artist, writer, or good at math? —And now you actually believe them?

Self-confidence isn't something that just happens after reading one blog or one book or even watching an empowering TED Talk. Self-confidence (like critical thinking, communication or writing skills) is a skill that develops with time and effort. *You must practice self-confidence. You must drill self-confidence into your psyche so that it becomes part of your "habitus"—your personality structure, your intuition, values and disposition.*

You must believe you are worthy. You must believe that your failures will not define you forever; you must believe that showcasing your vulnerability will not destroy you.

What's your disposition right now? Confident? Self-doubter? People-pleaser?

If you're not a naturally confident person, you need to work on building and strengthening your confidence as diligently as you pursue your career, financial and fitness goals.

A lot of people have NO self-confidence at all, so it's okay to get out of your comfort zone in smaller, incremental ways.

So how do you get some self-confidence?

- **Start small.** Voice your opinion in a meeting or classroom; join a book club or social group, etc. The more often you choose to go ALL IN, the greater the chances for success.
- **Remember that confidence is a growth mindset.**[36] You must believe you can grow your confidence, and you grow it by acting on it. Stop thinking and start acting.

- **Please stop RUMINATING.** Stop dwelling on your mistakes and previous experiences that were failures. That's all in the past: live in the past and you'll never achieve your future goals.

- **Stop hanging out with losers.** These people will sap you of the energy and motivation needed to better your life. They don't understand you and will actively try to dissuade you from achieving success. You will never get self-confidence from these types of people, so stop trying and start hanging out with winners.

- **Move past your failures quickly.** As soon as I fail at something, I take 10 to 15 minutes (OK, more like an hour!) to figure out what went so disastrously wrong, then I make a game plan to try again by changing things up. And then I MOVE ON. Do not allow failures to have power over you; do not internalize them.

Here's an example from my own life. When I got rejected the first time from the Master's program, I immediately (after wiping away the tears) made an appointment with the chair of the sociology department to find out the exact steps I needed to take to increase my chances of getting in. I then took more courses to raise my GPA, got another research job to enhance my skills and wrote as often as I could to better my writing. When others told me "Maybe it's not meant to be, Maja," I responded, "No. It just wasn't meant to be *right now*. But I'll get in and I'll succeed."

When I got rejected the second time, I can't lie, that one friggin' stung. I called my girlfriend in the middle of a shift at work and just cried on the sales floor at Holt Renfrew. But I vowed to try again next year with an even better application.

Yeah, I got into graduate school

I succeeded.

You can too.

Success is an option for ALL of us. We can't let failure keep us down.

Build Your Self-Confidence

Building self-confidence requires practice. What?! Did you think you were naturally supposed to be confident? Don't be a fool. You need to BUILD confidence. It's a growth-trait, meaning you can grow your confidence with practice. Some people seem to have more confidence than others. Maybe they're extroverted and love taking center stage. BUT the remaining 90% of us have to build it up!

HOW DO YOU BUILD CONFIDENCE?

1. PREPARE. You must train like a friggin' athlete. Train like an Olympian, like a UFC fighter. Train like a triathlete, train like an Ironwoman, train like Serena Williams or Ronda Rousey. Seriously, you will NEVER get better without practice. You think Tina Fey and Amy Poehler are just naturally funny? Or did they bust their asses for years working stand-up and improv so that they had the skills to back up their confidence?

Increasing your confidence isn't just about you, it's also about getting others to believe in you (which is integral to ANY job, ANY career, and ANY profession).

2. YOU MUST PRACTICE WHAT YOU FEAR. It's all about preparation and mastery. (You never just get up and give a speech, right? You prepare a speech, you practice that speech, you ask for feedback, you revise, edit, practice, and then perform that speech again.) That's what building your self-confidence is about. You must do the very thing that scares you. It's the only way out of mediocrity. For example, Dr. Jill Bolte Taylor practiced her inspiring TED Talk over 200 times beforehand. And her talk (*My Stroke of Insight*) has now been viewed over 15 million times. Practice pays off. Nobody just wings it.

3. INTERRUPT THE SCRIPT. Learn how to shut down that shitty committee in your mind, that negative voice, that annoying little doubter who's always creating fear in you. Unless you learn to silence that internal negative voice, you will lose out on vital experiences and opportunities and you'll be stuck, stuck, stuck, being ordinary and forgettable.

4. BE EXCEPTIONAL, EVERY DAY. What else can you do? DO MORE! How can you become better? Practice harder, practice smarter. Train. Ask for feedback. Have a schedule. Don't go for two-hour lunch breaks. Focus on your career, not what other people are doing. Make every single day count. Every. Single. Day. This is *incredibly* difficult, but you must fiercely guard every minute of your days.

5. STOP TAKING THINGS PERSONALLY. *It's not always about you!* If you get challenged by your boss, don't shrink away. Rise to the challenge and engage in debate. You're not going to be fired for voicing your opinion. Just because your boyfriend hasn't texted you back doesn't mean he's breaking up with you. Just because your best friend never returned your phone call doesn't mean she hates you. People are busy. And . . . it's really not all about you.

6. STOP TRYING TO BE LIKED, AND START FOCUSING ON BEING RESPECTED. I like a LOT of people, I respect a lot fewer. I get along with everyone; I'd only hire a select few to be my teaching or research assistants. Respect for people's intellect, communication skills and work ethic always wins out in the end. It's never about being liked, it's about being respected.

At the beginning of every day, at the end of every night you must believe in yourself. You must believe you are capable and worthy and deserving of success . . . and then you must outwork everyone else around you to ensure your success.

There is no other way.

Barrier #5

Mindset

"Why the f**k not me?"
should be your motto.

—Mindy Kaling,
Actress, comedienne,
best-selling author

By being aware of what
influences and derails your
mindset, you can stay on
that consistent path!

Body Talk

Body talk or, more specifically, fat talk is any disparaging dialogue about your body or weight. These can either be negative comments ("I hate my stomach") or positive ones ("Ugh, thank goodness I lost weight so now I can fit into my skinny jeans!").[37]

Fat talk is a contagious type of conversation that most girls and women engage in. If we're not directly disparaging our bodies, then we listen to other women do it. We participate in conversations that focus solely on our bodies, not our minds.

Fat talk is really about wanting to be someone other than who you are right now. Fat talk is the OPPOSITE of feeling empowered and having confidence.

Fat talk leads to negative internal dialogue such as: *"I wish my nose was straighter ... my hair curlier ... I wish I was taller, skinnier, blonder, tanned ... I wish, I wish, I wish. I wish I was different."* Because for some reason you think your life will be better if only you could obtain those things.

Right now, stop and think about how often you engage in these types of conversations on a daily basis. How often do you negatively comment on your appearance?

☐ Hourly
☐ Daily
☐ Weekly
☐ Monthly
☐ All. The. Time

These conversations occur among women all the time. At parties, in the hallway, on the bus, in the grocery store, at the gym, in line at Starbucks, and definitely in the change room of The Gap or Forever 21. We use fat talk as a way to gain validation from our peers, in the hopes that they'll say "Oh, no, you're not fat." We also use fat talk to fit in.

The more often you hear fat talk, the more likely you'll engage in it, and the greater the chances you'll really start believing this nonsense.

We are obsessed with our bodies and social media only fuels our insecurities. Our quest for the thin ideal[38] has narrowed our range of topics of conversation to our bodies. But we are more than just our bodies. We are more than our skinny jeans, our fad diets and kale smoothies. We can be more than the latest celebrity cookbooks or patchouli-mint scented candles.

TIPS

- *Never, ever fat talk in front of your children.* It's damaging beyond belief.
- *Stop comparing your body* and your features to other people's. (I know—it's easier said than done.)
- *Turn fat talk into career talk.* Start talking about other more important issues with your friends. *We are capable of discussing issues beyond food, nutrition, diet, our bodies, and skinny jeans. Let's talk about fulfilling our potential, working on our dreams and hanging out with women who inspire us, not just women we want to look like.*
- *Participate in the "Friends Don't Let Friends Fat Talk" movement*[39] which aims to replace negative talk with more useful positive affirmations. When you hear fat talk among your friends, you *MUST INTERRUPT the talk* (or what we like to call the "script"). Acknowledge the destructiveness of this type of dialogue and then change the topic to your career!
- **Recognize that fat talk is harmful.** It leads to body shaming, body dissatisfaction and disordered eating behaviors.[40] It's a sad fact that 90% of girls want to change some aspect of themselves, only 4% of women consider themselves beautiful and 60% of women withdraw from life activities because they're uncomfortable with their appearance. [41]
- When you get a compliment, don't deflect, don't self-deprecate, *just say "thank you."* And if you need comedic convincing, watch Amy Schumer's video "Compliments"—a valuable use of three minutes of your day.

Stop Talking about PMS!

I've noticed a trend over the past few years: women of all ages and areas of life discussing PMS. No one seems to be telling these women the truth. So here it is: Shut up with the PMS talk! No one cares, no one wants to hear it, and unless you're literally birthing a baby in front of someone, no one cares about your "cramps."

This is one of my pet peeves and definitely a career mistake so many women make. Just because I'm a woman doesn't mean I'm more inclined to listen to your sad story of PMS. Guess what? We all get PMS and we all go to work and contribute to society without (1) coming in late or handing in something late, or (2) calling in sick.

Nothing shows you're not ready for leadership like complaining about your PMS, or, even worse not completing a task because of your PMS. *It is NEVER appropriate to not do your work because of PMS, ever.* Take some damn Midol, people, and finish your work.

Sharing too much information can come back to haunt you the next time you're up for a promotion, negotiating a salary, or asking for more responsibility at work. If you're too stressed to handle your own bodily processes, how will you handle a job promotion or greater responsibilities at work?

I'm not saying you should never reveal personal information about yourself—we're not robots—but you must be selective in what you choose to reveal to your colleagues. You have to know *what type of information to share.* I'm not going to hide the fact that I'm a mother, but I'll never use my daughter as an excuse for not getting my work done.

If you're complaining about your PMS, I don't want you on my team, and neither will anyone else.

Welcome the Haters!

Do you know any haters? Ever feel badly about yourself or your dreams because of the haters? Let me explain something about haters. Haters are gonna hate. That's their job. Some haters will turn their hate to envy then eventually admiration and they'll become your biggest supporters. But many will continue to hate.

The more successful you become, the more you embrace change, the more positive you are, the more confidence you embody, the more haters you'll have. And that's OK, because at least they know about you and what you're doing. The worst-case scenario is not hate, it's obscurity. Nothing good happens in obscurity.

Haters are afraid. They live in fear of failure and are too scared to come out of their comfort zones. Haters are threatened by your success because it forces them to re-evaluate themselves and where they are in life. It's not about you. It's about them.

Successful people crave change. They look for new opportunities, challenges and risks. Successful people want to learn new skills, educate themselves, read, figure things out, absorb and create. Never forget that successful people take action.

Successful people are proactive. Haters are reactive.

Just remember, your haters will grow in number as you become more successful. It means you're moving in the right direction.

Haters use common phrases and passive-aggressive comments to bring you down. Following are a few examples:

- *Are you sure you want to do that?*
- *Aren't you a little too old for that?*
- *That's too risky.*
- *Why are you taking so long to finish school?*
- *Why don't you get a regular job?*
- *Why are you never satisfied with what you have?*
- *You're being greedy/aggressive/pushy/opinionated (etc.).*
- *Why can't you just blend in/get along/keep your opinions to yourself?*
- *You can't do everything.*

- *How will you balance your career with children/running a house-hold/pets/partner/spouse/family obligations?*
- *Why would you do that?*
- *What if you fail?*
- *You don't have time for that.*
- *You don't have enough money to do that.*
- *It's too late to try that.*
- *You don't have enough experience for that.*
- *You're not smart enough/good enough/strong enough.*

Embrace the support and love you get from others. Discard the hate. It's that simple.

The Imposter Syndrome

Does any of this sound familiar to you?

- *I can't believe I got into university/graduate school/medical school/law school.*
- *I can't believe they actually hired me/promoted me/made me manager.*
- *I can't believe I'm here because I don't know what I'm doing.*
- *I can't believe they asked me to talk, I don't know anything.*
- *Someone is going to find out I shouldn't be here and I'll get kicked out/demoted/fired.*

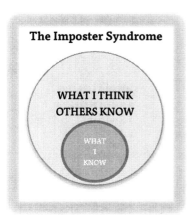

We usually talk ourselves out of taking a risk because we're scared and our self-doubt rages. We feel like we don't have enough or know enough. Even the most successful women suffer from the imposter syndrome.[42, 43]

Some of these excuses stem from believing that we're not good enough, smart enough, rich enough, have enough experience, or that it's not the right time.

Don't get me wrong. Self-doubt is part of life and part of the process of pushing beyond your comfort zone. But taken to an extreme, self-doubt is debilitating, and morphs into imposter syndrome. Women are plagued by it, but we can shift our mindset. Follow these tips.

TIPS

- *Learn to FAKE IT UNTIL YOU MAKE IT.* You must project confidence all the time, until it becomes second nature for you.
- *Practice, practice, practice.* Never stop learning. Never stop acquiring new skills. Most important, practice your public speaking and communication skills. Join a social club, book club or debate team. Take every opportunity to speak in public.

> **I know that failure is always on the table, so I feel the fear and I do what I need to do anyway.**
> —*Arlene Dickinson, owner and CEO of Venture Communications, co-star of Dragons' Den*

- *Develop a script.* What does your elevator pitch sound like? Can you sum up your brand, your thesis or grand idea in 30 seconds or less? Develop a 30-second, two-minute and five-minute pitch. Then say it aloud to a group of people and get some feedback. Revise and practice again.
- *Make your pitch concise, clear, and compelling.* Shape your message as a *solution* to a problem and start off with a headline, something provocative to grab their attention.
- *Fear and doubt never go away, so you must learn to overcome them.* We can't let them ruin our lives.

Winning Miss Congeniality Will Get You Nowhere

Why are SO many women obsessed with being "nice"? Why are we acting grateful when we should be acting confident? Because we're PEOPLE PLEASERS!

Why are we so timid, passive and fearful of interrupting or offending, when we should be putting ourselves and our ideas out there for everyone to hear?

Listen, ladies, winning Miss Congeniality will get you NOWHERE. Oh, wait— Actually it will get you somewhere. It will make you a people pleaser and a door mat. It will make you average, ordinary, and mediocre, but also completely forgettable.

Is that what you want?

Today I saw a woman receive the wrong order at Starbucks and instead of returning it, she said she *"didn't want to seem rude."* A colleague of mine last week accepted *another project* at work even though she had no time, simply because she doesn't know *when* and *how* to say *"No, I can't do that."*

> **Being nice is about being invisible, replaceable and forgettable.**

Being nice will not get you greatness. OK, I'm not saying you should be an asshole, but come ON! Being nice is insufficient for success. Being accommodating is not enough to achieve your fullest potential.

We've got to break this socialization pattern that's ingrained in us. We've been coached since toddlerhood *to be nice, to not interrupt, to wait our turn, to make friends and to be helpful.* Ugh.

Can you imagine how awesome it would be if all you ever heard growing up was:

- *How many times did you fail today? Fantastic! Tell me what you learned from your failures.*

- *Dreams don't work unless you take MASSIVE amounts of action. So what did you work on today?*
- *Taking risks is really important. Try it. Start small.*
- *Get used to living outside your comfort zone. That's where greatness lives.*
- *How much time are you spending working on someone else's dreams, instead of your own?*
- *What gives you joy?*

Did you know that after a divorce, a woman's standard of living DECLINES by 27% while a man's increases by 10%?[44] If you were divorced or widowed, how would you financially care for yourself and your family? Do you think you can pay the bank with homemade meatloaf and a sprinkle of niceness? Try it!

Ladies! Could we please stop worrying about being liked and being nice, and start working on our careers, making more money and living our dreams? And on that note, *STOP BAKING STUFF FOR THE OFFICE!* —No joke! I know so many women who bake things for their office mates or boss. If you have time to bake cookies and scones and pies, then you're not prioritizing your career. Because no one gets promoted based on baking skills unless they're actually in the food business.

Damn Girl, Let It Go!

My friend Brian recently ran into someone he hadn't seen in years. Even though this person hadn't bothered to show up to his wedding, send a gift or even RSVP, Brian went out for a beer with the guy. I, meanwhile, was busy making voodoo dolls. . . .

I once saw two guys get into a physical fight and the next week they were back to being friends. That would NEVER in a million years happen with women.

Ever notice that men just let things go, and women can hold on to resentment forever? Damn girls, we need to let that stuff go.

Holding grudges is toxic. When negative situations arise, there's always a lesson to be learned. Figure out what that lesson is, and then move on.

TIPS

- *Promptly handle the situation or person that offended you. NEVER let resentment fester.* It will only grow worse. (Why do women hate confrontation so much? It isn't some physical battle—it's just a conversation; you're confronting the issue, not the person).
- *Stop complaining* about other women or family members (I know! Easier said than done, Maja). But seriously, we all have a choice. We can accept the situation or person for what they are, or *change how WE react to them.* But replaying the past on an endless loop in your mind will only make the wound fester. It's a never-ending cycle of drama-hurt-ego-more-drama.
- *Stop expecting perfection from yourself and others.* No explanation needed.
- *Stop over-thinking the situation.* Just because someone didn't respond to your text right away doesn't mean they hate you.

Just because someone didn't call you back or their email seemed harsh doesn't mean they think you're an idiot. Stop the obsessive-compulsive negative thoughts; it's just noise in your mind that will distort your thinking.

- *Wishing people and situations were different is useless.* The past is already gone, so just focus on the now, the present and let your resentments go.
- *Stop blaming your parents or your shitty childhood for your life.* You're an adult now. Accept total and full responsibility for your failures and successes.

> There is an expiration date on blaming your parents for steering you in the wrong direction; the moment you are old enough to take the wheel.
>
> —J.K. Rowling

Every single one of us knows another woman (maybe even ourselves) who is holding on to some resentment, some internal crap or bizarre disagreement with another woman, friends or family. And we need to let it go.

Damn girl, if we're going to run the world we have to start thinking and behaving like LEADERS, not scrappers, not complainers, not petty little nitpickers.

Leadership in all areas of our lives is the goal here, not perfection, not people-pleasing, and certainly not living in the past by holding onto resentment and animosity. Hang out with like-minded women who are driven, ambitious and inspiring. Support this coalition of strong women and let go of the rest.

Limit Negativity in Your Life

I want to create, I want to be energized and impassioned and negativity just brings me down.

Negativity comes in many forms: online comments (oh my goodness, the trolls come out in full force); crime shows or real-life murder-mystery stories; family and friends who drain your energies; your own internal negative voice; even the news. I can't handle the barrage of depressing stories about gang rapes, animal cruelty, children left in cars, random stabbings and mass shootings. It's too much.

TIPS

- *Take inventory* of where the negativity in your life comes from (TV, technology, family, job, neighbors).
- *Associate with people who are more successful than you.* Their energy and positivity will help boost you up. Who are these people? Write their names down. Don't hang out with losers who drain your energy.
- *Recognize that some negativity you will not be able to change* (dealing with a medical emergency; a family member who is sick; taking care of elderly parents or grandparents; an ill pet; an intense volunteer job; financial stress)—SO, you must ADD more positive moments and energies into your life to balance out the intensity of the rest of it.
- *Meditate*—even if it's just for two minutes. Just sit in stillness (even though your mind may be racing), let the thoughts come and just sit and breathe. You'll feel so much better. You need some calm stillness in your life every day. Take a few minutes for yourself to do this.
- *Exercise.* Being active gets the feel-good hormones racing. You just feel better after exercising. My drug of choice is running. After a good run, I feel like I can do anything, seri-

ously! At the end of a 10k run I feel like I could run for mayor, start another company or rescue another Great Dane! This is the type of energy I try to harness for the rest of my day.

- *LAUGH.* I watch 15 minutes of comedy every day. It feels SO good to laugh, doesn't it? Netflix has a steady stream of standup comedians, and then there's the Comedy Network and obviously anything with Tina Fey, Amy Poehler, Amy Schumer, Mindy Kaling, or Louis C.K, Aziz Ansari, Bill Burr, Jim Gaffigan, Chelsea Paretti, or Tig Notaro.

How can you add more positive energy to your life? Ideas include meditation, exercise, yoga, reading, decluttering your home or workspace, and having a date night. For a great book on decluttering your life see, *The Life-changing Magic of Tidying Up: The Japanese Art of Decluttering and Organizing* by Marie Kondo. And for a great *parody* of this book, which also deals with getting rid of the negative junk in your mind, see the hilarious book *the life-changing magic of NOT GIVING A F*CK: how to stop spending time you don't have with people you don't like doing things you don't want to do* by Sarah Knight.

The Problem with Positive Thinking

Ever read the book *The Secret*? It was one of the biggest self-help books ever published—translated into 50 languages with over 20 million copies sold.[45] Its basic premise is that *like attracts like*. If you think positively, you'll attract positivity in your life.

However, one problem with these books is the promotion of false hope—the promotion of dreams without action. The most egregious omission is that *The Secret **never mentions WORK.***

Lots of people are ill, financially struggling or stuck in jobs they hate. But they can't just wish it away. You can't just think positively and hope that things will work out differently. Life doesn't work that way. If it did, I would be sending out positive vibes for 50% off BCBG every time I walked by their store.

These kinds of books aren't telling you the truth! IF you want a better life, a different career, or more money, you NEED TO WORK—harder and longer than you ever thought possible.

No amount of positive thinking will get you a different life if you don't work for it. If you want to get into graduate school, become a lawyer, doctor, engineer, artist, teacher, veterinarian, writer, business owner or developer, guess what? You gotta work!

Yes, I believe in thinking positively. —I don't want negativity in my life. *BUT you need to combine positive thinking with unimaginable levels of action, determination and persistence to become successful.* Unless you just want to be average; in that case, go ahead and read *The Secret* and tell me how that works out for you.

I tell my clients all the time that they need to think like winners, like superstars, and that they need to believe they are worthy and capable of achieving success and fulfilling their potential. BUT I then immediately follow up with a long discussion about combining positive thinking with a DIRECT ACTION PLAN. And then take action. Get to work!

You need to create action in your life and stop living in your mind, blissfully thinking positive thoughts. Start working. Start creating, and then start evaluating your actions. Keep track of your progress.

TIPS

- Next time you're wishing things were different, or daydreaming about winning the lottery—catch yourself! STOP and ask yourself: *What action have I taken today to advance my life? What quantifiable, measurable action have I taken to move me ahead in my quest to reach my full potential?*
- Success does not happen TO you. Success happens because of the sustained and deliberate action you take on a daily basis.
- Success will not drop into your life after you've sent enough positive thought-waves into the universe. You must create your success through your work ethic. Now get to work!

Erase "Luck" from Your Vocabulary

If I hear one more woman say "I'm just lucky I got this job" or "It's just sheer luck I got that raise" or "It's total luck that I got into graduate school," I will kick them! I swear I will.

Ladies, listen to me. Stop attributing your hard work, your skills, your talents and results to something so nebulous and external as "luck."

Ever hear a man say it was just luck that landed him a new client, raised profits or managed a crisis? Noooooo, it never, ever happens.

Because women externalize success and men internalize it.[46] Research consistently shows that men attribute their success to their inborn talents and skills. Meanwhile, women always want to mention "the team effort," or give others the credit. It makes me want to throw up. (OK, not really throw up, but you know what I mean, right?)

Who do you think gets the top leadership positions? The people who constantly reference "luck" and "chance" and how "lucky" they are to be where they are? OR the people who own their success, the ones who confidently state their accomplishments and their talents?

You must stop acting grateful for the position or job you're in, and start promoting yourself, start acting like you deserve to be there. The first step is by removing the word "luck" from your vocabulary.

Next time you're hanging out with your friends, make a note of how often women use the words "luck" or "lucky" to describe their current situation. Now that you're aware of the problem, you'll start to notice it everywhere, ALL the time. So when one of your friends says they're "lucky," I want you to interrupt and ask them why they need to externalize their success. Ask them if they've ever heard a man attribute his success to luck.

It may seem innocuous, but it's not. It's part of a larger, more systemic problem with women and their internalization of failure, as well as their overwhelming fear of reaching outside their comfort zone. If we constantly attribute our success to something external, not linking it directly to who we are and what we're capable of, then we'll continue to live in the comfort zone of mediocrity. We'll continue to not reach for things, not ask for raises or promotions, because it was only "luck" that got us there in the first place, right?

> **You may still have your fears, still battle with perfectionism, but know that you will overcome them when you put in the work and go ALL IN.**

No one changes the world
who isn't obsessed.

—*Billie Jean King,*
tennis player

3

Going
ALL IN

Step #1

Change Your Mindset

Choose people who lift you up.

—*Michelle Obama*

When Things Don't Go Your Way

When you're feeling overwhelmed with life, school or work, that little voice in your head—that negative voice that always doubts you—can play havoc with your self-esteem.

Here are 20 strategies to help you stay focused and motivated on the bigger picture: fulfilling your potential!

1. *Take ACTION.* Even if it's baby steps, take some type of action to keep moving forward. Never just do nothing. It's debilitating.

2. *Always aim higher—raise your goals and expectations.* Though things may not have worked out for you in this particular case, don't lower your ambitions.

3. *Hang out with a better crowd of people.* Be conscious and selective of whom you spend your time with, because you feed off other people's energies. Hang out with negative people all the time and you'll start feeling negative, too. Hang out with average people, and you'll start thinking average is just fine.

4. *Compete with yourself.* Avoid comparing yourself to others. Instead, ask yourself: "Am I fulfilling my potential every day? Did I do my absolute best today?"

5. *Focus on the now.* Keep it simple. Don't let your mind wander down that rabbit hole of hypothetical situations. Focus on the task at hand, the project or paper you need to write, not the fact that you're behind schedule or don't have all the resources you need.

6. *It's ALL on you.* Recognize that no one is going to swoop down and rescue you. It's literally ALL on you. If you want a better life, it's on you. If you want a better job, a better career, more money or success, it's ALL on you. Once you realize this, once you can see that you have the power to change your life, you'll feel free.

7. *Feel your emotions, but limit the pity party.* It's awful when things don't work out and you get rejected or fail at something. Acknowledge your emotions, but recognize that you are NOT your emotions. Have a short pity party and move ON.

8. *Always focus on the priority.* When things go awry, keep your focus. What's the bigger picture? Always go back to the ultimate vision you have for yourself. Working on your dream is tough, and you'll go through extreme exhaustion, pain, rejection, failure and then—eventually—success. Just keep your eye on the ultimate prize.

9. *Find multiple sources of support.* Lean on your mentors and supporters for help when you're down. But don't expect everyone to be as enthusiastic and supportive of your passion as you are; that's just unrealistic.

10. *Rephrase your inner negative voice.* Whenever you find you're being harsh or overly negative with yourself, immediately rephrase these negative thoughts into something positive: "I'm good enough." "I can do this." "I'm smart enough." "It might be tough, but I'll finish the project." That negative voice is just mind noise; recognize it for what it is.

11. *Believe in yourself and your capabilities.* You must internalize the belief that you can survive your mistakes and thrive. Women tend to behave in ways that are identical to how they see themselves. If you think you're worthless, you'll behave that way too. You think you're not smart, you won't make smart decisions. If you think you ARE your mistakes, then every time you fail it's another confirmation that you suck.

12. *Write it down.* Write down your vision, your dreams, and, most importantly, the daily goals that will help you achieve your fullest potential. Write it down and read it aloud every morning and every night. Do this! Don't just do it in your mind—write it down!

13. *Accept that sometimes completion is better than perfection.* Sometimes you just need to finish something. It might not be

pretty, it might not be your ultimate best, but finish it. Just complete the task! At times you have to aim for completion, not perfection. Lingering in the perfectionism-trap will paralyze you. It will limit your creativity, your energies and eventually lead to self-doubt.

14. *Don't overcomplicate things.* Keep it simple. You don't need to figure out your entire life right this minute. You just need to finish this paper, or write a blog, or work up the courage to do a cold-call for your business. Focus JUST on the task at hand. You don't have to have everything figured out to keep moving forward.

15. *Check for constructive feedback.* Constructive criticism is meant to help you, not harm you. Get used to asking for and being open to feedback from others. Why are you not succeeding with this particular project? Why are you struggling with this issue? Talk it over with someone who can provide new insight into your current struggles.

> **The difference between successful people and others is how long they spend time feeling sorry for themselves.**
>
> —*Barbara Corcoran, businesswoman, investor, speaker, consultant, syndicated columnist, author, and television personality on ABC's* Shark Tank

16. *Meditate.* The science surrounding meditation is undeniable. Take a few moments for yourself, be in the silence, let go of your thoughts, your emotions and just be still. It can clear your mind, energize you and change your negative thought patterns.

17. *Build your self-confidence by training.* Confidence is a skill that takes time and practice to fully develop. Just like critical writing or thinking skills, all it takes is practice, practice, practice.

18. *Find the joy.* When you're struggling with obstacles in your life, focus on the things that bring you joy to pull you out of your funk. For me, it's running or exercise. Even just going out for a quick 3k run resets my mind and spirit. It energizes me. I'm a health nut, so holding the plank position for 90 seconds actually makes me feel like a bad-ass warrior.

19. *Stop complaining.* When things don't work out, you have three choices: (1) Accept the situation for what it is; (2) Do nothing (and wish things were different); or (3) Change things up. There are real-time consequences for any of these choices. But you do have a choice.

20. *Focus on results, not effort.* Just because you worked hard, put in a lot of hours, or "really tried your best," doesn't necessarily mean it's good enough. Keep focusing on the results you get, not just the effort you're putting in. If you're not getting results after sustained effort, you might need to re-think your strategy.

Stop Ruminating, Start Reframing

Women ruminate. You ruminate, I ruminate. We THINK too much and too often about our mistakes and failures. We let them replay in our minds endlessly for hours and days, and sometimes even years.

We let our mistakes hold us back from stepping out of our comfort zones again and taking risks. According to Susan Nolen-Hoeksema, Ph.D., a professor of psychology, over-thinking is when you "go over your negative thoughts and feelings, examining them, questioning them, kneading them like dough."[47]

Over-thinking is different than basic worrying. Worriers worry about things that have NOT happened. They worry about hypothetical situations. Over-thinkers ruminate about things that have already happened. Worriers worry about the future while over-thinkers worry about the past. Over-thinkers are like worriers on steroids because they spend ALL their time stuck in the past, incapable of moving forward with life.[48] These thoughts have the ability to influence and change our behaviors.

If you don't manage or contain your negative emotions, they amplify.

For instance, when you're sad, worried or anxious, your brain tends to think about more sad events. You look through a distorted lens where you see every situation as hopeless, creating even more anxiety or worry for yourself. One thought leads to dozens of other thoughts that make you sadder or more anxious.

When you're in this state of mind, where you're over-thinking everything and your negative thoughts are amplifying, you tend to make poor decisions. You're not thinking rationally. You're thinking with your emotions.

Over-thinkers become paralyzed with their fears and doubts, because the only images they have of themselves are ones in which they've failed, made a mistake or let themselves and others down. They keep replaying this memory, this image of themselves until they're utterly convinced they are incapable of success.

When you over-think, you employ a negative lens to view your past. You see everything through a polluted, melodramatic and distorted lens. But remember: Things are not what they appear.

The good news is you can stop this. Read my tips to stop over-thinking on the next page.

How to Stop Over-Thinking

- *You must act deliberately to REFRAME your thinking.*[49] You must consciously interrupt the negative script in your head. Every time you find yourself ruminating, STOP. Take a breath. Redirect your thinking.

- *Remove your emotions from the analysis.* You need to objectively analyze why you failed without any emotion. Pretend you're analyzing this failure for a colleague. (For some odd reason, we're kinder to our colleagues and friends than we are to ourselves).

- *Practice, practice, practice.* Just as it takes time to better your public speaking or writing skills, so, too, does it take time to reframe that negative voice in your head. You have to practice increasing your emotional resilience. Be kinder to yourself. If you've been thinking like this your whole life, you won't dismantle these internal barriers overnight. Practice.

- *Change the scenery.* When you fail and you can't stop thinking about it, change your environment. Go into another room, or take a short drive. Go for a walk outside. Grab an overpriced tea or coffee at Starbucks. Go to the bookstore and browse the aisles. Try meditating or yoga. Do something else, something different to get your mind off the ruminating downward spiral.

- *Police your thoughts.* Recognize the triggers that cause you to over-think. Interrupt the negativity in your mind. (Are your triggers certain people, environments, anniversaries, times of day, conversations, or constantly comparing yourself to others?)

- *Distract yourself.* Immediately change direction and distract your mind by doing something different. Get down on the ground and do 15 push-ups! Hold the plank position for 30 seconds. Go for a walk. Read something that gives you joy (my go-to is always poetry). Watch something funny; laughter is so healing.

- *Give your pity party a time limit.* Feel sorry for yourself, play the victim, and over-think everything, BUT only do so for a very limited amount of time. Give yourself no more than 15 minutes (a day!) to be lost in this abyss of negativity and discontent. Then MOVE ON.
- *Use your support team.* Do you have a person or support team you can go to? Lean on a friend, colleague, partner, spouse, or mentor who will listen to you but also motivate you to move through the negativity. Join a social club that inspires and motivates you to succeed.
- *Start a gratitude journal.* This is an Oprah Winfrey idea. Every night or once a week, write down five things you're grateful for. Re-read these when you're feeling down, to show yourself how far you've come, how much you've accomplished and how totally capable you are of greatness. Over the years I've saved all the lovely emails and cards I've received from my students, and when I'm having a crappy day, I just re-read a few of them to remind myself that I'm not an asshole, that I do good work, and I actually help people.

Victim Mindset

When things don't go your way, who do you blame? It's rare to meet someone who admits, "Sorry I'm late—I honestly just left the house late." Instead, they'll say "Sorry I was late, but traffic was a mess, there was construction everywhere, and my GPS wasn't working."

I've heard every single excuse for late essays that you can think of. Every single year at least five grandmothers die simultaneously during exam week.

At some point, you just have to own where you are.

You have to own your mistakes, your failures and your current situation. That's part of maturing into an adult, although grown-ass adults come up with excuses all the time, too! They blame their childhoods, their parents, their spouses, their kids, their jobs, their lack of time, their education or their lack of money.

> **You control your results.**
> **You control your actions.**
> **It's ALL on you.**

Blaming others is part of having a victim mindset and occurs when you look for the easy way out. You blame anybody and anything BUT yourself. This mentality develops when you carry unresolved resentment, anger and discontent within you.

You always, always have a choice. You can take responsibility, accept accountability and learn from your mistakes and failures, OR you can blame everyone else for your lot in life. Why blame what you cannot change? You have no control over how your parents raised you. So why try to blame something that you cannot control?

The only thing you can control is YOUR thinking, YOUR mindset, YOUR actions, and YOUR responses. Focus on these and let go of the rest.

I know the haters are going to come out for this chapter, but— Successful people don't have time for excuses, while people who play the victim thrive on them, because that's ALL they know.

The only thing that feeds excuses is more time. You're giving your excuses too much time to get bigger and have even more power over you. Stop thinking about why you're unhappy with your life, and ACT NOW! Do something about it! To achieve real success and fulfill your potential, you have to be prepared to accept complete accountability for your life—where you are right now and where you're going.

People have difficulty letting go of the victim mindset because some part of them is still invested in it. Some part of their mind or spirit still derives rewards or benefits from the excuses. Whether by deflecting attention away from the real problem or trying to avoid judgment or even failure, you're invested in your excuses and they feed your victim mentality.

One of my favorite books is *The Power of Now: A Guide to Spiritual Enlightenment* by Eckhart Tolle. This is what he says about playing the victim:[50] "To complain is always non-acceptance of what is. . . . it carries an unconscious negative charge. When you complain you make yourself into a victim. . . . So, change the situation by taking action, leave the situation or accept it. All else is madness."[51]

You—only you—are responsible for your emotions and your actions. And you either pollute your mind (and your environment) with your negative thoughts, excuses and complaints, or you add passion and enthusiasm.

It's your choice. Pollution or passion, which will you choose? *You control your results. You control your actions.*

TIPS[52]

- If you want a different life, then *do things differently.* Take a different route or a different action. You can't keep doing the same thing but expect different results.

- *Stop feeling sorry for yourself.* Oh, this is a tough one, because everyone enjoys a pity party. Especially when things don't go well. I used to really like shopping when I had a bad day. "Charge it!" (Oh, how Visa loved me!) —But that's not really a viable solution. Give yourself a 15-minute (OK, 30-minute) pity party. Watch something funny on Netflix or YouTube and then MOVE ON. Pity parties must have an end to them.

- *Associate with accountables.* Who do you hang out with? Do they enable your pity-party behavior? Are they willing to listen to you making excuse after excuse as to why you're the victim and don't have the life you want? You don't need those people. What you need are people who are willing to hold you accountable. You need people willing to be honest and call you out on your crap. My husband Steve is my accountable, and he's on top of my work like mad. At times (OK, lots of times) it irritates me and stresses me out, but without his constant prodding and pushing to do more, produce more, write more, I probably wouldn't have written this book (certainly not this quickly).

When you start blaming others—STOP. Readjust your thinking. RE-FOCUS back to your long-term vision. Then realign your daily goals to make sure they're connected to that long-term vision.

Beware of Mediocrity

Being average won't get you noticed. Being mediocre means you're ordinary. Who wants to be that? Being average is nothing special at all.[53]

Here's a dictionary definition of "mediocre": "not satisfactory, poor, inferior; barely adequate; neither good nor bad; undistinguished, pedestrian, everyday, run-of-the-mill, meager, low-quality, second-rate."

Can you imagine someone saying in a job interview—

- *I can give you an average effort.*
- *I would describe my potential as mediocre.*
- *I can definitely contribute to this company in an undistinguished manner.*

Yeah, sounds ridiculous. You wouldn't get the job. Who wants to hire average? Who wants to be associated with common, ordinary or second-rate people? NO ONE does!

> **Most people live "in the average." Don't be like most people. Be extraordinary. Live there. Breathe there.**
> **Exist only there.**

If you want to get noticed, get promoted, sell your product or your idea, then you have to be extraordinary; you must be better-than-the-rest. You must kill the competition with your brilliance. Stop thinking about doing just enough, and start working on being phenomenal, outstanding, unprecedented and incredible. That's what will get you noticed.

In everything that you do, every step you take, every project you handle, do these things:

- *Over-deliver on everything.* Your competition will do the bare minimum while you need to do everything necessary to blow them away. Over-deliver.

- *Always say "yes" to every CAREER opportunity* (even if you don't feel like it or it's a lot of work or you don't get paid for it). Think of the bigger picture. Look at every experience as a career opportunity to network and self-promote. You may not see the financial benefits right away, but still say "yes."
- *Master your craft.* Whatever you're doing, be the best. Be exceptional, do exceptional work. Be known for your exceptional work ethic and results.

Most people live "in the average." Don't be like most people. Be extraordinary. Live there. Breathe there. Exist only there.

Always Say "Yes"—to Yourself

If you come from a "Place of No," you'll end up middle-of-the-pack with the rest of the people who are content to be average. If you want to excel, stand out, and be successful, you'll always say yes to new opportunities, new experiences, and new challenges.

BUT you must distinguish between saying "yes" to yourself and your career and saying "yes" to everyone else. Put yourself first, put your career first.

Typically what happens with women is that *they start worrying about hypothetical situations* that might never happen. Women worry about whether they have the skills to do this, the time to do that, whether they have enough information, or even if they're the right person for the job.

Then women start over-thinking the situation (this is when you're fixated on stuff that happened in the past). You start ruminating on your failures and mistakes, replaying them over and over again in your mind until you're either depressed or convinced yourself you're not up for the task.

When I was an undergraduate student, my university mentor asked me to be on his research team. I was so shocked that he believed in me and thought I had something of value to add that I immediately started giving him reasons why I wasn't the right candidate! Can you believe this?

This is what I said:

"Are you sure you want me on your research team?"

"Aren't there more qualified people than me?"

"How can I work with graduate students when I'm only an undergraduate? They'll think I'm an idiot."

"I don't know what I could contribute. I haven't even finished my degree."

"Are you sure you think I can handle this?"

"What if we're researching stuff I've never learned about or know nothing about?"

Just typing this up makes me cringe with embarrassment. I was basically telling him why I wasn't qualified. He's the professor, he's got the Ph.D., he's the one with the research grant, he's the boss, and he wanted me on the team. He knew what he was doing, and this was my response. Pitiful! Never again.

Working for him taught me SO many valuable lessons.

- *Always believe in yourself.* Even when you're scared out of your mind, you must fake that confidence until it becomes natural.
- *You can figure it out later.* Always say "yes" to different opportunities, and figure out how you'll do it afterwards. Why, why, WHY do women feel the need to have it all perfectly figured out ahead of time? This is a perfectionist attribute that is so harmful to your career and your mental health. Just say "yes," and then figure it out as you go. Learning on the job is almost always more beneficial than having "book smarts." I learned more in my various research positions than I EVER learned in school (and I have a Ph.D.!) Learning as you go is just what positive successful people do. It took me a while to figure this out.

Over the years, whenever I was presented with a new task, something I'd never done before, I always said "YES":

- *Yes,* I'll learn that new software program.
- *Yes,* I'll interview gamblers even though I've never conducted a qualitative interview before. Yikes!
- *Yes,* I'll apply for graduate school, even though I might not get in.
- *Yes,* I'll keep applying for grad school even though I got rejected last year.
- *Yes,* I'll be a teaching assistant, even though—holy crap—will students listen to me?
- *Yes,* I'll teach a class, even though I've only ever been a teaching assistant.

- *Yes,* I'll manage four teaching assistants, even though I've never done it before.
- *Yes,* I'll teach a class of 250 students, even though I'm used to only 80 students.
- *Yes,* I'll teach a new course even though it starts in two weeks and it's not in my core area of expertise.
- *Yes,* I'll apply for a post-doctoral position researching homelessness and addictions even though that's not my specialty and everyone complains about how difficult it is to get post-doc positions and I'll probably not get it—but OK, I'll try.
- *Yes,* I'll learn that new software—in my new post-doctoral position. Bam!
- *Yes,* I'll publish papers, and yes, I'll present at conferences, and yes, I'll start a new company, and yes, I'll write a book. . . .
- *Yes, yes, yes, yes, yes, yes, yes, yes, yes, yes, yes, yes, yes!*

SAY YES. You'll be continuously rewarded by being a life-long learner.

SAY YES until you're so successful and so busy that you have to say no. But until then, keep promoting yourself and your brand or ideas and say YES to everything. You never know when the next great opportunity will arrive. Be prepared by being everywhere. Be seen. Get noticed. (And you better have your elevator pitch perfected!)

Invest in Yourself

Success doesn't just happen. You must train for it. You must develop an aptitude for it. That's why you need to invest in yourself.

When is the last time you spent money on your career? Most people spend more money on entertainment or their wardrobe than their careers. Have you spent more money on your smartphone than your career? When is the last time you bought a book, attended a seminar, or got new business cards?

> **If you're not investing in yourself and your career, how can you expect other people to?**

If you're not investing in yourself and your career, how can you expect other people to? You need to treat your career, your success and your potential like the biggest competition of your life. Take this seriously by investing in yourself.

TIPS

- *Read* motivational and inspiring books.
- *Find people who inspire you and read their stories.* I gravitate towards strong, independent female leaders in all fields (comedians, CEO's, business leaders, athletes).
- *Assess how you look.* Do you still look like a student even though you've graduated? Time to update. But have fun with your fashion . . . don't look like everyone else.
- *How do you sound?* Ideally, you want to sound articulate and confident. So, read communication or public speaking books, and watch comedians to learn the art of delivery and timing.
- *Develop your writing skills* by writing often and asking for feedback. Then practice some more.
- *Listen to inspiring TED Talks* or other videos about the habits of successful people.[54]

- *Hang out with like-minded people.* Stop spending time with people who are 9-to-5'ers. You won't learn anything from them. You won't be inspired or motivated to do more. And more is what you need. You can always DO MORE. You can always work smarter; you can always train harder.
- *Read empowering blogs* (like mine!) on a daily basis to keep you motivated and on track.
- *Attend a career seminar, networking lunch or public speaking opportunity.*
- *Listen to audio tapes* in the car, while you're on the bus, or working out. I always listen to sales training CD's in the car to motivate me. I never listen to the radio or music unless I'm working out.

If you can't remember the last time you invested in your career, then it's time to invest. No one will do this for you, and more importantly, other people are already investing in their careers and they'll blow right past you.

Get rid of the guilt. You deserve to invest in yourself. Do NOT feel guilty for spending money on your career and on services or products that will help you fulfill your dreams.

You are worthy of success. Now surround yourself with things that motivate you to jump out of bed at 5 a.m. and work on your dreams.

Just Make a Friggin' Decision

Do you ask your mother, sister, best friend, boyfriend, girlfriend, colleague, neighbor and nutritionist for their opinions before you make a decision? Well, stop doing this! It's weak. It shows you're indecisive and lack confidence, and nobody wants a leader who's uncertain and insecure. Here's a perfect example:

> I had a student who asked for an extension. I had already given the entire class an extra week. But I granted her another seven days, making clear that if she handed the paper in after that, I wouldn't mark it. She handed it in on the eighth day. If I didn't mark the paper, she would fail the course and, since she was already on academic probation, probably get kicked out of university. This weighed heavily on me, and instead of *just making a friggin' decision*, I conferred with everyone.
>
> I asked my husband what he would do. I spoke to three academic colleagues. I asked my mother (who's a high school principal). I debated endlessly. I wasted SO much time trying to make "the right decision," and internalized the student's own anxiety and stress about failing out of school. I even spoke to the head of student accessibility (though the student didn't have accessibility issues) for 30 minutes (!!) about what endless extensions teach students. We spoke about the value of learning how to manage your time and the point of deadlines and the vast difference between university life and the real world. Ridiculous!!! I mean, just MAKE A DECISION, MAJA!!
>
> My gut told me I shouldn't accept that paper. But instead of sticking to my original decision, I wanted to be "nice" and didn't want to make the "wrong" decision. In the end, after way too much time debating it, I didn't accept the paper, because I wanted to be fair to the others in the class whose papers I didn't accept after the deadline. Her academic probation was on her, not me, and I had to learn to not internalize other people's dramas and mistakes.
>
> This was an important lesson for me to learn, because I've NEVER had a male colleague debate an issue like this. In fact, when I asked my male colleagues they looked at me like I was a fool. "Nope, don't accept the paper. End of story." "Why are you wasting time even thinking about this?" Yeah, why was I wasting so much of my time?? Can you imagine if I had asked my boss what to do? Canvassing for multiple opinions NEVER makes you look like a leader.

Moral of the story: Stop asking for everyone's opinion before making a decision. Women do this to avoid risk. While leaders lead, women hope "they get it right," so they can avoid blame in case they're wrong.

But it also happens because women suffer from perfectionism. Perfectionism doesn't ensure you're perfect; it just ensures you're stressed. In the end, you fail at doing it all, because NO ONE CAN DO IT ALL, or do it all perfectly.

Next time you need to make a decision: Just make one. If you made the wrong decision, so be it. At least you made one.

Ever go out with friends for dinner and find that more often than not it's women who say "I just can't decide what to eat," as if it's such a cute thing to be indecisive? Um, it's not.

Challenge: Make one decision today without asking anyone else for their opinion. At work, if you normally ask your boss before doing something, just move forward with the decision. Start off with a relatively low-risk decision and build up from there. Don't start by firing people—build up to that.

Remember, you're not a polling station. Stop canvasing people for their opinions.

Take Credit for Your Work

Learning to take credit for a job well done seems simple enough, but most women continue to make the career mistake of sharing credit with their colleagues. People don't get promoted because they're awesome team players; they get promoted because they have leadership qualities.

Women tend not to take credit for things for two reasons:

- They believe their good work will speak for itself.
- They don't want to be perceived as arrogant.

Let's start with the belief that good work should speak for itself. Women truly believe that others will simply notice the work they've done and congratulate them. THIS DOES NOT HAPPEN IN THE REAL WORLD.

When I was a makeup artist working for Bobbi Brown cosmetics at Holt Renfrew, I was a shark on the sales floor. I was aggressive and loved selling. I was also the top salesperson across Canada. Because of my high sales I was able to negotiate for more. More gratis (free makeup products), better vacation time, better hours (I LOVED working through my lunch and only taking a quick 15 minutes to eat—more time on the sales floor, right?). I negotiated for a bigger bonus, because I made sure EVERYONE knew about my high sales. From my fellow make-up artists to the managers, everyone knew how good I was at sales. I was proud of my numbers and wanted to make sure I was being duly compensated.

Women are regularly passed over for promotions because they didn't realize that getting noticed is part of the game—*and you need to play the game.* You need to let *everyone* know about your accomplishments—targets reached, profits earned, money saved, enrolments increased, or commendations received—because no one else will do this for you!

Being "nice" or "compliant" or "helpful" may be useful in grade school but it certainly doesn't get you to the top leadership positions in the work world. No one is watching in the wings, waiting to swoop down and congratulate you on your work and sing your praises to management. Management doesn't know who you are until you give them a reason to. SO, sing your own praises.

I've had women in my class who have accomplished major feats (published their writing, won awards for their academic performance, volunteer or community service, spoke five languages or were named to the dean's list), but they never wanted to speak of their success. They felt shy or humble about their achievements. Some of them didn't even think it was important enough to put on their cover letters or resumes! —This must stop.

Secondly, women don't want to seem arrogant. We're so worried about coming off the wrong way that we've internalized childhood cultural ideals of what it means to be a woman— women are nurturers, caregivers, helpers—instead of seeing ourselves as confident, capable and driven.

Collectively, we must become more comfortable with taking credit for our good work. We must recognize there is no shame in this, and there's nothing to be embarrassed about. In fact, you should be embarrassed if you miss an opportunity to tell others about your accomplishments.

Embrace Constructive Feedback

Don't you hate it when someone asks you for your opinion and then gets irritated with you when you tell them the truth?

Well, if you don't want the truth, then don't ask for my opinion. Sheesh!

But you know what? Most people have NO idea how to handle constructive feedback. They take it as a personal attack on their character; they start shutting down or wildly defending themselves. Are you one of those people?

You can tell immediately when someone can't handle criticism, because the excuses start flying out:

- *"This is just a rough draft."*
- *"I'm not finished yet."*
- *"I'm not an expert on this."*
- *"I can't be expected to know it all."*
- *"I'm just starting out."*

Yeah, SO? You asked me for my opinion and I'm telling you that you can be better, your ideas can be sharpened, and your product needs to be fine-tuned. Doesn't that help you, not harm you?

This is where you see the difference between successful people and those doomed to a life of mediocrity. Because being open to constructive feedback is an uncomfortable place to be in, and if all you want is comfort, then all you'll know or be is ordinary.

Hearing that your ideas aren't that great is a humbling experience but more than that, it's an opportunity for growth. When I was in the final stages of this book, I met with my editor, David, and he gave me pages of suggestions for revisions. THIS IS FANTASTIC. Revisions will ultimately make my book better. Then I'll send the book out to a few colleagues for their valuable feedback and critiques. Feedback is awesome! Use it to your advantage; don't get emotional about it.

A student came to see me about her paper. When I explained everything that she needed to improve upon, she started crying. I asked her if we should stop, and she said "No, keep going. I need to hear this, because everyone tells me my work is great but I can never get anything higher than a B+. I want to know how to get an A." Weeks later, she came back to see me and said, "Thank you so much for the feedback. It was difficult to process everything you were saying, but now I know what it takes to write an A paper. I wish I had known this earlier. I wish people would have just told me the truth, instead of just saying my work was great, when really it was just OK." She had a total "A-HA" moment. This girl is going places!

> **Those who seek out feedback are the unafraid. They are the ones who know the true value of change.**

Personally, all I want is to be better, to make my writing better, to present my lectures better, and to engage with more people. SO WHY WOULD I PUSH AWAY CONSTRUCTIVE FEEDBACK?

The next time someone gives you constructive feedback on your work do this:

- Meet with them in person (or by Skype) to go over the feedback.
- Say THANK YOU for the feedback.
- Listen. Don't defend yourself. You're not on trial.
- Ask how you can improve. What are the exact steps?
- Thank them again, and get another appointment booked for more feedback once you've worked on the existing suggestions.
- Go home and work on the suggestions without allowing yourself to wallow in self-pity for not getting something perfect the first time around.
- Then repeat these steps with everyone who is gracious enough to give you feedback.

Most feedback is truly constructive and meant to propel you forward. Be open to realizing you don't know it all, you're not perfect and there's always room for improvement.

Start working on your communication skills, which are invaluable assets in any career or business you venture into.

There is always something you can improve upon.

Giving Constructive Feedback

We live in emotional times and everyone is SO overly sensitive, don't you think? When I'm asked to give my opinion on something, or to give constructive feedback (when I'm marking assignments, for instance), I try to follow some guidelines to ensure that (1) I don't sound like a jerk; and (2) my message pushes through their emotional state of mind.

CONSTRUCTIVE FEEDBACK GUIDELINES

- Always start with something positive. No one wants to hear you rip into them right from the get-go.
- Go into *specific details* about what needs to be improved upon. Don't be afraid of hurting someone's feelings—just tell them what didn't work well. Use examples where necessary.
- Keep it concise. This shouldn't be a 30-minute discussion or a two-page email. Keep it short, to the point, factual and not emotional. Don't overwhelm the person with feedback.
- Suggest one or two main things the person should work on. Again, be as specific as possible.
- Keep your tone and language professional. Don't apologize for how the person is feeling or reacting to your feedback. Hearing the truth is more important than living in ignorance.

Stop Waiting for Opportunities. Create Them

Do you wait for opportunities? Do you wait for great things to happen to you? Or do you create opportunities for yourself wherever you are?

I used to wait for opportunities. I used to think my hard work and discipline would get me noticed. I used to think that just because I had the highest teaching scores or students loved me or spoke highly of me, that I would get noticed by someone, somehow.

Then I WOKE UP!

I realized I needed to create opportunities every day with everyone I met. That's partly why I started my blog and ALL IN club. I was tired of waiting for great things to happen to me, and started creating momentum for myself so that I produced the conditions that CREATED GREAT THINGS.

I took responsibility for my lack of success and recognized that I hadn't worked hard enough. I had underestimated the HUGE amount of effort and dedication it would take to achieve my potential.

Ever hear people say, "Oh, the economy is tanking, there are no jobs, no one is hiring," or "I've applied for 10, 20, 30 jobs and no one has called me back"?

The problem isn't the economy. The problem is you. I know it sounds harsh. But when you evaluate everything you've done so far, and compare it to everything you could have or should have done, you'll see there's a huge gap.

What should you do? **DO SOMETHING, ANYTHING AND DO IT NOW.** Stop waiting around. Don't over-think it, just do it.

Back in the day, when I was a (wannabe) makeup artist, I desperately wanted to work for M.A.C. but didn't have any formal makeup artistry training. BUT I did have a boatload of passion, and was extremely knowledgeable about their products (because I spent all my money on makeup and owned 60% of their line). So one day I walked up to the M.A.C counter, asked to see the manager and introduced myself. I started off with the positive: "Hi, Suzanne, nice to meet you. My name is Maja, and I'm M.A.C's biggest fan. No one knows more about these amazing products than I do. And even better, I love to sell and I have a lot of sales training and experience." (Notice I didn't mention the fact that I didn't have artistry training. NEVER lead with the negative). Then I ASKED for the job. "I'd love to work for M.A.C. How can we make that happen?" (Again, I didn't ask a yes or no question. I forced her to explain her answer.) She gave me the typical response: "Oh, we're not hiring right now. Oh, you need to have a certificate in makeup . . . blah, blah, blah."

Then I made her an offer she couldn't resist. A risk-free trial. "How about I work for you for the entire day for free? All I'll do is makeup. Prom makeup, evening looks, smoky eyes, you name it, I can do it. You assess my makeup skills and if you think I suck, then I'll go home, no questions asked. BUT if you think I'm awesome, which I am, then you'll give me a job. Deal?" —They were slammed with prom business and understaffed. She took a chance on me and for the next seven hours straight (with no breaks) I did 24 full makeup looks.

Oh yeah, I also got a three-month contract ON THE SPOT at the end of my shift. She said she was amazed at my enthusiasm and that no one had ever asked for the job in the way I did. She was impressed. And I was on Cloud 9 because I just landed my dream job! I didn't wait around and politely apply to the HR department. I created an opportunity. There was nothing to lose; worst-case scenario was that she'd say no. And then I simply would have driven to another mall and another M.A.C. location until I got a "Yes." I was determined.

Whether it was working at M.A.C. or starting my own business, I stopped thinking about it and just jumped in. Now it's your turn.

Be Ambitious, Not Grateful

You must develop a leader's mindset, a leader's lingo, a leader's confidence.

Men are aggressive in pursuing what they want, **while women typically hold back.**

Men see and seize opportunities wherever they are and with everyone they meet, **while women wait for permission.**

Men are constantly looking for their next promotion, **while women talk and daydream about it.**

Men are always visible; making sure everyone knows who they are. **Women want to blend in, sit at the back and go unnoticed.**

Men ask for challenging assignments; they always ask for more than they can handle. **Women wait to be asked, assuming their work ethic will get them noticed. Guess what? It never does.**

Men look for opportunities to showcase their leadership qualities while women talk about team work.[55] **(Ugh!)**

Men are constantly selling themselves as capable, driven, dedicated, and ambitious. They see themselves as leaders. **Women think self-promotion is too brash, too cocky or aggressive, so they sit on the friggin' sidelines.**

Men are always thinking about their next career move. **Women are fearful, driven by that stupid negative voice in their heads that tells them they can't do something, so they stagnate in mediocrity.** Or worse yet: Women usually have NO idea where they want to be five years from now. They don't envision themselves as leaders, winners or successful. Some even struggle to identify their skill sets.

Successful people think like leaders. Unsuccessful people think like followers.

Women are cautious *and men are forward thinkers.* **Women want to play by the rules to make sure they don't offend anyone.** *Men take charge and worry about the consequences (if any) later.*

Of course, not every man is this confident and not every woman is this passive. But the research confirms that in general this is the sad difference between how men and women think about themselves, how they promote themselves, and how they approach their careers.[56]

Remember that M.A.C job that I landed? Well, fast forward a year, and I was looking to work for an artist-driven line. I wanted to work for Holt Renfrew (Canada's most prestigious retailer), and I did exactly what I did with M.A.C. Armed with my resume I walked into the Bloor Street location, right up to the Bobbi Brown counter, and asked for the job. I led with the positive: "I'm a passionate seller with M.A.C makeup experience. But now I'm looking to work for an artist-driven line. How can I help you out?" The district sale manager was there that day, and interviewed me on the spot. I was aggressive in my sales pitch. "I was M.A.C's number-one seller in units-per-transactions, and I never took lunch breaks. I love selling. I can't wait to start selling for Bobbi Brown." The district manager LOVED my pitch. She said, "No one has ever asked for a job like you. You're different. Most girls just drop off their resume and walk away. When can you start?" I kid you not, I got the job THAT DAY. I distinctly remember calling my boyfriend (now husband Steve) and saying, "Can you believe this? I just walked up to the counter and asked for the job, and I got it! —It was that easy."

When she gave me the contract, I made sure to negotiate for a dollar more per hour, extra vacation time (I was getting married in December, which was the biggest month for sales), and a larger bonus based on my sales. I was ambitious. Not grateful.

The question for you is: When will you step up? When will you shut down that negative voice? When will you stop doubting yourself? When will you be willing to take a risk, fail at something and then get BACK UP? When?

Stop Being So Humble

Ever compliment a woman on a recent achievement only to hear her say:

"It's not a big deal, everyone wins these things."

"Oh, it's not really me, it was my team."

"Oh, it was nothing."

"Oh, I couldn't have done it without help."

"I don't even know why I won this award/scholarship/grant; there are so many other talented projects/people/ideas out there."

Men *own* their successes. Women *downplay* their achievements.

When men fail at something, they attribute it to something external. ("The course wasn't taught well." "The material just wasn't interesting.")

When women fail at something, they attribute it to something internal. ("I'm not good at math." "I'm not smart enough.")[57]

Ask a man why he succeeded at something and watch him take ownership of it all.

Ask a woman, and watch her attribute her success to everyone but herself—her team, her assistant, her students, friends, colleagues, hairdresser, or the neighbor down the street—basically, everyone but her.

Guess who sounds more confident, more assured, more knowledgeable? Guess who's going to get hired and promoted?

TIPS

- *Never, ever, ever downplay your achievements. Ever. Death to downplaying!* Never insinuate that it was anyone else but you PRIMARILY who got the job done. Yes, everyone wants to work with team players and you've got to get along with others. But you'll never stand out and achieve your fullest potential if you think you need a whole team to get you there.

- *Say "Thank you."* When you receive a compliment, say "Thank you!" —That's it. You don't need to justify your success; you don't need to explain that others helped you. All you need to say is "Thank you." Anything else makes you look apprehensive. You start creating doubt in people for no reason.

- *Self-promote.* Start turning your achievements, milestones and successes into opportunities for re-branding and networking. Everyone should know about your successes; why would you hide this?

- *Pay it forward.* The next time you hear another woman downplay her achievements, take her aside and ask her why she does this. WE need to create a coalition of strong, intelligent, and confident women. Let's help each other out (what a typically "nice" thing to do, right?)

Maja's accomplishments

Wrote book in 5 months

Started a blog

Started a YouTube channel

Ran a half-marathon

- *Write down a list of your accomplishments.* Review this list every time you're feeling doubtful. (It doesn't matter how short your list is at this point—everyone has accomplishments). Keep this list in your wallet.

What Are You Feeding Your Mind?

What are you reading? What are you listening to? Who are you spending time with?

All of these are influences on your mindset, your thoughts, your attitudes and your energy levels.

You must be conscious and deliberate about what you're feeding your mind.

I simultaneously love and curse Netflix. I have lost hours upon hours—OK, who are we kidding, I've lost an entire week of my life binge-watching Scandal, vicariously living through Olivia Pope. But I could have put those 40 hours into my career. Sacrifices must be made for the greater good.

Put down that *Glamour* magazine. Turn off Netflix, and stop watching clips from *The Tonight Show with Jimmy Fallon*.

On any given day you have the opportunity to lean into your fullest potential and create success, or you can waste your time. It's your choice, and you make these choices every hour of every day.

What are you listening to on the car ride home from work or school? What's playing on your iPhone when you're riding public transit? Music? Movies? Or material to keep you motivated and on-track to achieve success?

What book is on your night stand? When's the last time you learned a new word? My personal favorites include *plethora* and *serendipitous*. I read the dictionary. I know that makes me an ultra-nerd to a degree you didn't think possible, but it's true. I study the dictionary. I secretly get excited when I come across words I can't pronounce or have never heard before. And thank you to Merriam-Webster's online dictionary with its audio pronunciation app! All you have to do is click a button to hear the correct pronunciation of strange words like *trammel*, *solecism*, and *obscurantism*.

Everything counts, all the time. Keep feeding your mind material that inspires you, encourages you, and informs you. (And makes you laugh!) You're never too young or too old to be more aware of what you're feeding your mind.

> Right now I'm teaching Ryo all the different words to describe being surprised. She knows *shocked* and *flabbergasted* and *pandemonium*. And she's three. But I speak above her current level, because I expect MORE from her. Every week we learn a few new words. Last week it was all the different words for "big" (*huge, humongous, enormous, gigantic, large, massive*). Next week we're on to synonyms for "different" (*unique, special. . . .*)

TIPS

- *The learning never stops.* The average Fortune 500 CEO reads five books a month. The typical North American adult reads one book a year![58] Yup. That's not a typo. CEO's read five a month, average people read one a year. That's sad. The average CEO makes 331 times the average worker's salary and 774 times as much as a minimum wage worker.[59]

- *Reading stimulates the mind.* According to Emory University's latest study, reading has positive long-term effects on the brain.[60]

- *What's trending in your area?* Read or listen to podcasts about everything related to your industry. What's the competition doing?

- *Stay motivated.* When you're facing a barrier, stay motivated by reading or listening about those who have succeeded in your field. Read their memoirs or how-to books.

- *Invest in your career by buying books.* Don't worry about the $25 you'll spend, worry about missing key info in that book that will push you further along. Successful people invest in their careers by reading and by attending seminars, conferences, and networking opportunities. Unsuccessful people just worry about the cost of these things, or spend weeks looking for them on sale. Don't discount the power of books to keep you motivated.

- *Set a target.* Read one book a week or listen to three podcasts a week. In the past two weeks I've read a book about spirituality, one on raising toddlers, and one on the entrepreneurial life. You must set a target for what you'll read next. My target is 50 pages a night. I carry a book with me at all times and I'll read every chance I get. Standing in line at Costco, the grocery store or the bank. I love reading. Turn off technology and just read. Enjoy.

Women Hating on Women: This Has to Stop!

Stop trying to tear down other women. Stop complaining about other women and how they dress, sound, look or act.

As women we're bombarded with obstacles and barriers to our success—our gender, sexuality, race, ethnicity, social class, and so on. We do not need more barriers.

There are SO many external barriers women face that we cannot have infighting. We must support each other. We must recognize that one woman's success does not diminish other women's capacity for success, but increases it.

Stop looking at other women as your direct competition, and start acting like a coalition.

By diminishing other women's accomplishments, we're diminishing all women and the greater cause: more women leaders; more women bosses; more women in politics; more women in Parliament; more women in finance; more women in positions of power and authority.

I recently had tea with a new colleague and told her about the ALL IN mindset and how as women we need to help each other out. I encouraged her to reach for a new job just outside her comfort zone. I sent her job postings when I came across something that suited her. Her response told me all I needed to know. She cried. Someone in your field (especially another woman) showing you kindness, support and encouragement should NOT be such a rare occurrence that it causes you to cry. That was a sad moment for me, and I also cried. Because, I didn't want to be the first woman to help her out; I should have been the twentieth or fiftieth woman helping her, because we should all be looking out for each other.

Can women be sexist toward other women? Absolutely. There's a real difference in the way women speak about male entrepreneurs and their drive for financial success as *forward-*

thinkers, as opposed to what we say about Martha Stewart or Bethenny Frankel (describing them as *greedy and overly ambitious.*) As women, we internalize these gendered cultural ideas of what women should want in life and how they should go about achieving it.

We like women who are successful—just not too successful, right? WRONG. This must stop. More women achieving success is what we want. More women leaders are what we want. More women presidents and prime ministers, more women CEO's and CFO's are what we need.

TIPS

- *Look for opportunities to praise* other women's' accomplishments and use it as a networking opportunity, instead of trying to take down another woman,
- *Become part of a social club* or group where you'll interact with like-minded women and support the hell out of each other.
- *Disengage from the negative talk* and don't bad-mouth other women. Walk away from the gossipy conversations or change the topic. Rise above the gossip. We're better than that.

Step #2

Change Your Work Habits

Life is hard; complaining rarely improves things.

—*Karen Finerman, CEO of Metropolitan Capital Advisors and CNBC panelist*

Life Begins at 5 a.m.

Ever wake up at 8 a.m., 9 a.m., or (shockingly) even later than that? Well, you're wasting your life. No joke.

You can be so much more productive by starting at 5 a.m.!

Every day I aim to get up at 5 a.m. I fail and sleep in at times, BUT the goal is 5 a.m. and I'm getting there. As soon as I get up, depending on the injury-state of my ankles/knees/shins, I'll either run or do a weight training program. For me, exercising in the morning is the key to a good start to the day. It means I've taken time for myself which allows me some quiet time to think about my day, develop some ideas or just zone out. Either way I'm recharging myself and my energies.

Waking up at 5 a.m. means I'm ahead of the day, right from the start. It's about being proactive, not reacting to the day's events because I fell behind. Early risers feel more productive, energetic and accomplished. It's the only way to maximize your efficiency and keep the momentum going. Feeling proactive is intimately tied to our level of coherence (feeling in control) and the more in control you are, the more confidence you have, the more you empower yourself.

TIPS

- *Figure out your schedule.* If 5 a.m. is out of the question for you, then be prepared to stay up later...it's one or the other. You won't achieve success without sacrifices; you either get up early or go to bed late. Figure out what works for you.
- *Understand why you need to start early or work late.* (Hint: It's linked to your personal vision and life goals.)
- *For early risers, avoid caffeinated stimulants* after a certain hour and go to bed earlier.

Work at Extraordinary Levels

If you want to push through the noise, if you want to stand out, you need to work at insane levels of productivity. You must work every single day toward your dream, your vision and fulfilling your potential.

If you're not putting in extraordinary, unbelievable, uncommon levels of work, then you're not working enough!

You must do what others are unwilling to do.

You must get up earlier than others.

You must outwork others. Kill it with productivity, not just being busy.

You must stretch yourself completely out of your comfort zone. You must take a risk.

You must have such a passion for what you do that every single day is work, and YOU LOVE IT.

I work every single day because I absolutely love, love, love, love, love what I do. I can't imagine doing anything else.

Do you have a mentor? I have a bunch of mentors (mostly women) and most of them I've never met. But I admire their careers, I admire their work ethic, and I read everything I can about their rise to success, their daily schedules, their obstacles and how they overcame them.

Whenever I get frustrated (which happens often) I look to my mentors and get inspired by their tenacity and their determination to succeed.

It took me a while to figure this out, but nothing worth achieving in life will be achieved on a whim. Success doesn't happen instantaneously or haphazardly. Success occurs when you're outworking the rest of the field.

Looking back on my graduate-school days, I can see how I wasn't working at ridiculously productive levels every day. There were phenomenal weeks or months where I was producing work at incredible levels, but the rest of the time it was merely mediocre or average or ordinary levels of work

If I had only worked at insane levels all the time, I would have certainly accomplished more. I would have dreamed bigger. I would have aimed higher.

That's what extraordinary levels of work do for you. They make you realize just how much more you can accomplish, and that there is no limit to your success.

Work at insane levels and you'll start to see success "happen for you." People will comment that "things always go your way" or "you're so lucky" or "you're an overnight success." But you and I both know there's no truth to any of that.

The truth is, the harder you work and the smarter you work, the more success you will achieve. More opportunities will open up for you, and things will become easier for you.

Try it and I guarantee it'll work.

Try to work at extraordinary levels for 66 days straight and see how much further you've gone, how much closer you've come to your dreams and your ultimate vision for your life. Why 66 days? Well, the average length of time it takes to form a new habit is NOT 21 days as the fluffy self-help books would tell you.[61] Breaking in a new habit (like learning to work at insane levels) takes TIME, upwards of two months of consistent daily action! Don't be scared off by this 66 number. You can do it.

Aways Over-Deliver!

Whatever job you're in, whoever you're working for, always, always OVER-DELIVER. You must outwork your co-workers and colleagues in order to get noticed.

But there's NO POINT in over-delivering if you don't tell everyone what an amazing job you're doing! Don't believe that mythical idea that "the work will speak for itself." NO, IT WON'T! I must shout this at you, because most women make this egregious mistake again and again. Stop waiting to get noticed. It doesn't work. While you're waiting, 12 other people (mostly men) are charging ahead using a megaphone to scream their accomplishments.

Wherever you are in life, you must go ALL IN, ALL THE WAY, ALL THE TIME. Half-measures do nothing. Even if you're working full-time, raising kids, taking care of the household, you can still work on your dreams. It'll be a longer haul, but that doesn't mean you shouldn't do it.

Whatever project you're working on, commit all the way. Don't "just try it out." Because just trying something out, just dabbling, will never produce exceptional results, and exceptional should always be your target. You want to live and breathe and swim in the exceptional waters. OK?

Over-delivering helps to:

- *Emphasize dependability.* People know they can rely on your extreme work ethic. They know your word means something and that you'll always make your deadline.
- *Produce exceptional results.* People come to expect greatness from you and your work because you've always delivered your best work at all times.
- *Show initiative and confidence.* When you're producing exceptional work on a consistent basis you look more competent, you feel more confident, and people love your drive, your instinct and initiative. It's contagious. AND people feel

confident recommending you to others. This is how you get future (and continuous) employment.

- *Show you're motivated.* You're motivated to learn, grow, and to challenge yourself. You don't live in the past; you're always looking forward.
- *Create success.* Successful people don't just stumble upon success. They work at being successful, and with each little bit of success, more doors open for them, more opportunities come their way. This is not luck. This is preparation, dedication and perseverance.
- *Demand greatness of you.* By consistently over-delivering on your projects, you automatically push yourself further than you ever thought possible. Thinking outside the box starts to become the norm. Seeing challenges as opportunities is where you live now. You are able to distinguish between mediocrity and greatness, and greatness is who you are.

Over-deliver and you'll see success wherever you are.

I took a long time to finish my undergraduate degree—10 or 11 years, in fact. After first year, I immediately dropped down to two or three courses per year so I could actually learn something, instead of just cramming for exams, then immediately forgetting everything I'd studied. I took dozens of extra courses because I was genuinely interested in the material. I worked my ass off and eventually became a research trainee, then a research assistant.

Over the next 10 years I NEVER applied for a single research position! Every single research position I got through my contacts and the power of recommendations and referrals. Employers I had previously worked for, over-delivering exceptional work, recommended me to others. When I needed a new job, I emailed my previous employers and asked them for work. And work always showed up.

Because I always over-delivered, my colleagues knew they could count on me. They felt confident putting their own reputations on the line recommending me to others, because they knew I would always, without a doubt, be great at what I did. And I was, because I saw the value in over-delivering for myself and my bosses.

Empty the Tank

Creating a different life will require more energy, work, and persistence than you ever thought possible. You shouldn't go gently to bed. You should drop into bed utterly exhausted because you've emptied the tank and there's nothing left to give.

That's what *every* night should feel like: complete and utter exhaustion, but also exhilaration because you know you're closer to fulfilling your potential today than yesterday.

Taking your career to the next level is like taking your fitness to the next level. When I go for a run I have two choices: (1) go hard—run fast—go uphill; or (2) take it easy. It's the runs that make me want to vomit at the end that tell me I've emptied the tank. Those are the training runs that allow me to run faster in my next race. The easy runs? Those are just for recovery days—they let my body rest, but they won't get me first place.

If you feel good when you cross the finish line of a half-marathon, then you didn't empty the tank. You shouldn't even be able to stand; you should feel dizzy and sick to your stomach because you gave it everything you had.

That's how you should structure your days, so that by the end you're completely depleted, physically, mentally and emotionally.

Remember that student-lifestyle-mindset I mentioned earlier? Yeah, I fell victim to it too. I did not empty the tank each and every day. Had I done so, I would have accomplished more, and gotten closer to reaching my potential.

Learn to love the feeling of emptying the tank, just like you'll grow to love getting up at 5 a.m. (OK, the 5 a.m. kinda sucks for a while.)

Go ALL IN, all the way, all the time. Be truthful with yourself when you don't, when you still have something left in the tank, and correct this the next day.

What Are You Learning at Work?

You know it's time to move on from your job when you can't remember the last time you learned something new. So, what are you really learning in your job?

Don't think about the job; think about the new skills you'll acquire in the job. And when you've acquired those new skills and the challenge is gone, it's time to find a new job.

People don't stay in their jobs for 10 or 20 years anymore. It's all about growth.

If you don't like your job, leave. Don't stay in a position that you hate, working for a boss you loathe, doing something that doesn't stimulate or challenge you, when you have a choice.

And if you're in a tough situation and need the job because it pays the bills, then EVERY SINGLE moment outside of work should be spent on finding a new job.

Staying in a job past the point of pleasure is so depressing, and so mentally exhausting, it's just not worth the damage to your mental or physical health.

I've been in those types of positions and I've got colleagues right now working in jobs they can't stand and every day it kills them a little bit more to go to work. Every day, their creativity gets stifled, their ego gets bruised and the self-doubt rages on. One of the main reasons I left academic life and pursued an entrepreneurial course was because I knew I wasn't fulfilling my potential in academia.

My blog, my social club and this book are all centered on one thing: getting women to fulfill their potential! I want women to get out of their comfort zones and achieve outrageous amounts of success, and the only way to do that is to keep growing, keep challenging yourself, and keep pushing forward.

Working 9-to-5

If you've got a 9-to-5 job that you love and never take work home with you, then stop reading right now. But if you want to get out of your 9-to-5 rut, read on, my friend.

If you think working 37½ hours a week is going to get you your dreams, you're wrong.

If you think working 37½ hours will bring you closer to your ultimate vision for yourself and your life, let me tell you THIS WILL NEVER HAPPEN.

If you want greatness, if you want freedom (career freedom, financial freedom, creative freedom), then you need to work harder, smarter, and longer than anyone else. You need to RISE ABOVE THE CLUTTER that is the herd and start getting noticed.

You need to go ALL IN ALL THE WAY ALL THE TIME.

We all know people who say, "Oh, I always wanted to write a book," "I always wanted to be a photographer," "I always wanted to learn another language," or "I always wanted to go back to school." BUT then they did NOTHING about it.

Don't be those people.

Don't look back years from now, wishing you had done more, achieved more, and became more.

Working 9-to-5 on your dream is not enough. I have friends who put in 40 hours of work in three days. Guess what? They're a lot closer to their dreams than everyone else.

You need to go ALL IN, ALL THE WAY, ALL THE TIME.

That means:

- Saying "no" to a lot of things and a lot of people. ("No, I can't go to the movies with you, because I'm working on my dreams." "No, I can't go out for dinner with you, because I'm working on my business." "No, I can't help you with your project because I have to finish my work.") Get it?

- Getting rid of guilt because you said "no" to someone. Stop feeling guilty for putting yourself first. You need to take care of yourself FIRST—then you'll have the resources, time and energy to help others.
- Recognizing you need to work EVERY DAY on your dreams. You need to allocate every spare minute you have to getting closer to your dreams. Some days will be more productive than others. That's OK. Just keep going. Consistency is the key.
- Forgetting about "balance" for now. You can't be worried about leading a balanced life when you haven't done anything great yet. Start working on being great. That's your priority, not achieving balance.
- Recognizing your time wasters. Do you spend more time cooking, eating, cleaning, watching TV, shopping or gossiping than you do on your dreams? Then you're WASTING YOUR PRECIOUS TIME. While you're wasting time, you better believe someone else is maximizing their time and getting ahead.

WHEN YOU CAN'T QUIT YOUR 9-TO-5

Listen, I know most of us don't have the luxury of quitting our day jobs to work on our dreams. But that doesn't mean you have to save your dreams for the weekend or put them on hold altogether. You must work every day to fulfill your potential, even if it's only for an hour, even if it's just for 30 minutes.

Most people aren't working in their dream jobs or occupations, because they need an income to survive. You've got to pay the bills somehow, so don't neglect your paid job while you work on your dreams. You've got to keep that income coming in, but keep your passion alive by continuing to work on your dreams every single day.

Evaluate yourself: At the end of the day score yourself. Did you waste time OR did you maximize time? It's one or the other. Which one is it for you?

IT'S NOT ALL-OR-NOTHING. Just because you can't work on your dreams 100% of the time doesn't mean you should abandon them completely. Realize that most ultra-successful people still had to work their day jobs for a while before they could quit and focus on their passion full time. Most people have partners, children, family obligations, pets, and household crap to take care of that interferes with their actual work. Everyone has time constraints and financial issues, but that doesn't mean you should stop working towards your potential.

Keep going, every single day. Just. Keep. Going.

TGIF

Are you one of those people who shouts "TGIF!"? Do you look forward to the weekend so you can forget about work?

Every Monday people ask me, *"What did you do this weekend?"* and my answer is always the same. I worked, because I love what I do.

If you're talking about hump day or TGIF or watching YouTube videos at work, then you're not in the right job.

My job doesn't feel like work, because I have a passion for what I do. Monday, Thursday, Saturday, I can't tell the difference, because every day is a work day.

Every day I'm out there hustling to get noticed, to learn new skills, to write a blog, make a video, do a podcast, and to send something out there of value and substance.

If you have enough time to daydream about the weekend, wow, then you're not really living your life. You're just hanging out in some mediocre existence doing average things, leading an ordinary life which will only ever get you very uninspiring results.

According to a Salary.com survey, 69% of employees surf the net—on non-work related stuff. The most popular time wasters at work are Facebook, LinkedIn, Twitter and Pinterest. The #1 reason you're looking at these sites is because you're BORED and you're not challenged in your job.[62]

Hoping your life will be different isn't going to pay the bills. Living your life vicariously through beautifully staged and Photoshopped images on Pinterest will not get you those things.

You want a different life? Then start doing things differently. And then keep doing them, day after day after day. Spend more time actively pursuing your goals with such an obsession that people will call you crazy, as they're sitting at the bar on hump day complaining about work . . . and you're out there succeeding EVERYWHERE you go.

A lot of people are afraid to say what they want. That's why they don't get what they want.

—*Madonna, singer, songwriter, actress*

4

Communication Toolkit

Stop Apologizing
(Sorry If That Sounded Rude)

Stop apologizing. Seriously. Women need to stop apologizing for everything ALL. THE. TIME.

I see this happen in conferences, seminars, workshops, graduate school, with my undergraduate students, at work, in meetings, at the grocery store, or my daughter's daycare—everywhere I go, a woman is apologizing for something. I can't remember the last time I heard a man apologize.

Where there's a woman, there's an apology coming up shortly. This. Is. The. Truth. And it makes us sound like idiots. Who wants to take direction from someone who is constantly apologizing?

Leaders lead, successful people take ownership, and women apologize. We must change this.

This is what I've apologized for this week:

- Asked for more soy milk at Starbucks in my iced coffee and I apologized to the barista.
- Someone bumped into me on the escalator at the mall and I apologized to them.
- I said "excuse me" to move past someone at the grocery store and then I apologized.
- I walked into my boss's office and immediately said, "Sorry to bother you."

I say this to enrage you so that we stop apologizing. I encourage all women to interrupt this apology tour we're on.

Why do we constantly apologize?

Fear of not being liked. Fear of being seen as bossy, as overreaching in our desires or ambitions. We fear *sounding stupid,* so we pre-empt what we think people are thinking with an apology, as if to say *"I already know what you're thinking—and I'm sorry."* It's crazy talk. *We also desperately fear offending people.* Heaven forbid we should disagree with someone, or voice an alternate (or unpopular) opinion.

Don't apologize for: Wanting something. Being ambitious, talented, and intelligent. Don't apologize for thinking outside the box, changing things up, having opinions, or wanting to succeed. Also, don't apologize for wanting money! There's no shame in wanting financial success.

Don't apologize for seeking a different life from your parents, siblings, family members, friends or colleagues.

Don't apologize for not following the status quo. Don't apologize for following your passion.

The only thing you should EVER apologize for is not working hard enough at fulfilling your passion, and the only person you should apologize to . . . is yourself.

The first thing out of your mouth should not be an apology. It should be a sound bite about how awesome you are, or how fantastic your ideas, product or service is.

Get OFF the apology train.

Don't Over-Explain

When you're asked why a project wasn't completed, or why your paper was late, or why you deserve a raise, just answer the question with facts, not emotions. Don't feel the need to constantly over-explain yourself. Brevity is key. *When you speak you must project confidence and self-assurance.* Don't attach qualifiers to the start of your sentences. They distract from your overall point.[63]

For example, if your boss asks what went wrong with a project, the typical female answer might sound like this:

"Well, I'm not entirely sure, so I'll just offer my opinion. I don't want to speak on behalf of the group or anything. Or maybe I should. Would that be OK? Because I think we're probably all on the same page, at least I think we are. So, I think some of the mistakes—perhaps mistakes is too harsh a word—but some of the challenges certainly that we faced on this project were issues such as trying to reframe the overall vision of the department, along with perhaps not having all the information necessary at the time, so that it took longer than anticipated. [Blah, blah, blah . . .]"

Could you get through that passage? So long-winded, so passive, so apologetic, so verbose! Just state what the problem is and how you're going to solve it. This is what every professor, every manager, every leader wants to know. Problem and solution. That's it. Anything more and you're boring them, wasting their time, or making yourself look foolish. Seriously.

Now let's try answering that question again. Your boss asks what went wrong with the project:

"We had two key issues: (1) a lack of information necessary to help us re-frame the department's vision; and (2) we underestimated the time needed to complete the task." See the difference?

162

WHY DO WOMEN OVER-EXPLAIN ISSUES?

- Fear of sounding harsh, opinionated, or bossy.
- Fear of not being liked, so we soften our answer.
- Fear of being wrong, so it's better to sound unsure; then we can't be blamed for something. (Over-explaining distracts from our message and undermines our confidence and competence.)
- Not pausing before speaking; since we hadn't collected our thoughts into an organized answer, we just keep talking and talking and talking.

Here's what a typical woman sounds like:

"I'm not sure, but I think—"

"Perhaps we could try this way—"

"Maybe the reason this didn't work is—"

"I don't know."

"It's just my (humble) opinion."

This. Is. So. Frustrating. What is going on? No one knows! Because you're not definitive in your answers. You sound unsure of yourself, and that makes others unsure of your abilities and capabilities.

Switch passive statements like these for something like:

"We will do this—"

"I suggest we analyze the—"

"I know we were successful with this project because—"

"The project failed for three reasons—"

TIPS

- **PAUSE! Take a moment** to figure out your answer next time you need to explain or justify something,.
- **State the problem succinctly.** No emotions, just facts.
- **State the solution.** How will this problem be resolved?
- **Then stop talking.** That's it.

Please Start Asking Questions

Do you avoid asking questions for fear of standing out in a classroom or work setting? Do you think you'll sound like an idiot for asking a question? During every single lecture I tell my students: "Please ask me anything. There are no stupid questions. Your question will benefit others." But no one asks any questions. Or, to be exact, WOMEN don't ask questions.

And then they proceed to freak out because they don't know what they're doing. They

> **Asking a question is proactive. Coming to me afterward with your problems is reactive. See the difference?**

don't know how to use a particular system or piece of software, whether it's the library system, Excel, or PowerPoint. But still they stay silent. This is not just a problem with university or college students; this is a problem employers complain about, too.

What's wrong with just saying, "I don't know how to do that?" GREAT! Let's figure it out. Let me show you how, or direct you someplace where you can get help. Having a game plan is so much better than drifting off aimlessly into a stress-filled, anxiety-ridden abyss (a little dramatic for sure!). Believe me, you'll save yourself and your professor or boss a lot of grief, time and stress if you ask a question right away, rather than after a problem has occurred.

Asking a question is proactive. Coming to me afterward with your problems is reactive. See the difference?

You ask me a question right away because you need clarification and I think you're eager with a take-charge attitude. Come to me weeks later with your problems because you couldn't find the courage to ask for help, and now I think you're disorganized and lack authority. *Asking a question moves you forward. Keeping silent keeps you where you are.*

How to Ask a Question

When a woman asks a question during class, or in meetings at work, it starts like this:

"I'm sorry if you've already mentioned this, but—"

"This is probably going to sound stupid, but—"

"Sorry if someone has said this, but—"

WHAT is going on here, ladies?! How are girls going to "run the world," as Beyoncé says, if we start all our questions off with apologies and disclaimers?

But starting with an apology isn't the only problem. Ever listen to someone ask a question that goes on and ON and ON? People have asked me questions during presentations that were so rambling that I had to write them down and then repeat them out loud to make sure I understood what they were asking! I've also had to cut people off because they simply didn't know what they wanted to ask. I've even had to take the microphone away from people during seminars because they were so nervous they just kept rambling on.

When you ask a question at school, work, in the audience at a speech or workshop, or even on the phone or while leaving a message, follow these tips:

- Know exactly what you want to ask before you speak.
- Write your question down.
- Your question should be one sentence. It should take only 10 to 20 seconds to ask.
- Don't ask three-part questions. Everyone hates these. Two questions maximum per person, then they kick you out of the club!
- Never start your question off with an apology ("I'm sorry if you've already been asked this—").
- Don't start with a story, explanation, lecture or preamble. Get to the point. The quicker you get to the point the more con-

fident you sound. The longer it takes to ask your question, the more confused and disorganized you sound.

- After you've asked your question, stop talking! I can't emphasize this enough. Put the microphone down, take a seat, and then listen to the response.

TIPS

- **Count the number of times you apologize** before or after you've asked your question. Once you see how often this happens, you'll stop.
- **Even if you're catching yourself mid-word**, you must stop apologizing. Speak up when you hear other women doing this, too; we must help each other out, and awareness is the key.
- **Jot down your key points when leaving a voice mail.** Your message should NOT be longer than one minute. State your name slowly and clearly, state your question or concern, and then give your contact information. That's ALL. Do not give a story or history of your issues, just get to the point. Pretend your voice mail communications are court transcripts being read aloud. Do you sound like a leader? Or do you sound crazy?

Practice asking questions with confidence, because if you don't sound confident no one will have confidence in your skills or abilities.

Your Voice: Do's and Don'ts

- *Don't end statements on an upward inflection.* It makes you sound incompetent. Seriously. Are you asking the audience something or are you telling us something? Because the way you sound makes it seem like you don't have a clue.
- *Don't trail off. . . .* You need to finish your statement, and when in doubt: JUST. STOP. TALKING. When nerves kick in, you get flustered, start talking (usually quickly), have no idea what you're saying and don't know how to stop. So you trail off until you're inaudible. Stop this.
- *Don't speed-talk.* The audience is listening; they're trying to understand you; so give them the chance to actually follow what you're saying by not racing. The preferred speed for delivering a speech is the same pace you speak at in the normal course of conversation—on average, between 130 and 170 words per minute. Most people don't have a problem speaking too slowly. Instead, stress and nerves make them speed up. If you're prone to speed-talking, write "SLOW DOWN" on your speech notes, or time yourself beforehand so you know where you should be at each page of your speech.
- *Don't talk too softly.* Holy crap! No ONE can HEAR YOU. I have to shout this at you, because soft-talkers and mumblers are THE worst. If you're a low- or soft-talker, you need to SPEAK UP. Can you hear me?! Because no one can hear YOU, and when no one can hear you, that means people stop trying to listen and become disengaged. I've sat at conferences right beside a speaker and still couldn't hear her. I've been introduced to women and not caught their names because they spoke so softly. Speaking this way makes you seem ultra-fragile, like you're going to break into half if you project your voice. It also seems like you lack confidence. Learn how to project your voice. Speak as if you don't have a micro-

phone and need everyone in the room to hear you. When I've got a class of 75 or 100 students, I project so that someone in the far back corner can clearly hear me. (By the way, no one really wants soft-talkers on their team. It may sound harsh, but when you're working on a team project with a tight deadline, you don't want to waste time figuring out what someone is saying and constantly asking, "Can you repeat that?" After a while, people stop asking you, because they don't care anymore about your opinion. I've seen this happen dozens of times.)

- *Pause before you speak.* The next time you're asked a question, pause and breathe. Reflect on what your answer should be. Make sure there is an overall point to your answer. Without a pause you run the risk of saying whatever comes to mind, and then you start rambling on, forgetting your point. *Pausing before you speak showcases confidence.* Really, it does! People think that pausing before you speak makes you look unprepared or incompetent, but in fact the opposite is true. Pausing makes you look thoughtful, like you're taking the time to give the audience a well-prepared, insightful answer. Finally, pausing makes people perk up and listen more intently. When there's silence, people listen, because they think you're about to say something really important. It builds anticipation. It gets people's attention, and in public speaking, that's what you want.
- *Know your point or question BEFORE you speak* (whether in person or placing a call or leaving a voice mail.)

OK. Lecture is over!

Remember: Speak up or you'll get left on the sidelines, in school, in business and in life. Learn to speak UP!

Why We Hate Public Speaking

- *Nerves.* It's perfectly acceptable to be nervous before you speak in public. Most people have butterflies in their stomach beforehand. That's NORMAL. Having a healthy sense of fear is good.

- *Mistakes.* For some reason, we think that whatever we say in public has to be perfect, no mistakes or failures allowed. But this is just not possible. You will make a mistake or flub your lines or say something off-the-cuff that you probably shouldn't have. You will forget your point, lose your train of thought or tell a joke that completely fails. That's part of the process.[64]

- *Lack of preparation.* Make sure you adequately prepare. If you're giving a speech you must prepare for it. Don't try to wing it or ad lib. Not even seasoned professional speakers can do that. Everyone prepares. Barack Obama prepares his speeches. Bill Clinton practices his talking points.[65] If they're practicing, then OH HELL YEAH, we should be too.

- *Lack of practice.* If you want to get better at public speaking the only thing that will help you is to practice, practice, practice. It's that simple. Take every opportunity you have to say something aloud, talk to a group of people, ask a question in a class or work meeting. Volunteer to speak at an event. Offer your opinion. Practice using PowerPoint or including visual aids until you're proficient. Practice telling jokes until people actually laugh. It's all about practicing. If you really, truly want to become a better speaker, you must practice.

- *Reluctance to accept attention.* Women have a hard time accepting they're the center of attention. Just last week at the hair salon I heard a woman complaining about how much she hates being the center of attention—*at her own wedding!* I couldn't believe this woman. She had internalized the idea that women shouldn't speak up or get noticed because that would be arrogant. As much as it may scare you, you must push yourself to take center stage and believe that you have value to add.

Get comfortable with being uncomfortable

You'll never grow if you stay in your comfort zone. You'll never achieve your full potential if you constantly worry about what others think. You'll never achieve your dreams if you don't practice, practice, practice.

The more you stretch beyond your comfort zone and live in that uncomfortable zone where the butterflies and nerves run rampant, the easier public speaking will become.

Get comfortable with being uncomfortable.

Public Speaking Tips

Speaking in public is one of people's biggest fears. Some reasons include:

- *Everyone will laugh at me.*
- *I'll sound like a fool.*
- *I'll make a mistake.*
- *I'll get asked something I can't answer.*
- *I'll make a joke and no one will laugh.*
- *People will be bored; they'll be on their phones.*
- *Someone will post my mistakes on social media.*

If you want to sound better when you speak in public (in any setting) follow these tips.

TIPS

- ***Practice!*** You will not improve without practice.
- ***Do short drills.*** In my ALL IN social club we do quick-burst debates. Each person gets handed a topic at random and then has 10 seconds to collect their thoughts and then 30 seconds to present their views. After they've spoken, everyone in the room provides immediate feedback.
- ***Learn from your mistakes.*** Write down what went wrong and then work on overcoming those mistakes.
- ***Think like a warrior.*** Whenever my daughter mentions a princess, I say warriors are better, because a princess always waits for other people to help her out, but warriors can do anything they want. Think like a warrior: Believe that you will own this speech and this moment. Don't internalize the idea that you're not good enough to be speaking in public. Don't surrender your potential to these ingrained ideas of gender.
- ***Record yourself and review.*** Now that everyone has a smart phone, it's easy to get immediate feedback on how you look

and sound. Ask others for feedback. How are your tone, eye contact, gestures, and pacing?

- *Beware of fillers.* Eliminate words and phrases such as "um," "you know," "ahh," "oh," and "you know what I mean?" Silence is always better than fillers.

- *Get over the fact that at some point you'll fail.* Yes, your speeches will suck sometimes, but the important issue is what will you do about that? How will you learn from your mistakes? Will you keep trying? Don't become invisible just because you made a mistake.

- *Take every opportunity to speak up.* Ask a question in class or in a meeting. Disagree with something. Voice your opinion. Practice, practice, practice.

Here's an example of learning from your mistakes. The first year I was a teaching assistant I sucked. I didn't know what I was doing, didn't have any guidance, and didn't know enough to ask for help. The class didn't relate to me at all, because I didn't open up to them, and I was overly strict with crazy expectations for first-year students. BUT, what I did do well was ask for feedback. And when those 120 surveys came back, those kids let me have it. I'll NEVER forget the comment, "I think she's forgotten what it's like to be in first year. Please don't be so harsh to the next group of students." Ouch. Reading those reviews made me step up my game big time.

How Much Space Do You Take Up?

Often, women feel more comfortable stepping OUT of the limelight. They recoil instead of standing tall. They choose the backstage. They lean back, instead of leaning in.

What you have to say is as important as how you speak and how you present yourself physically.

Do you try to take up as much space as possible when you enter a room?

Your body language and how you present yourself are an indicator to others of how seriously they should take you.

> **You're always communicating something, even when you say nothing.**

Your posture, your handshake (stop with the limp handshakes!), your voice, and how you hold yourself can either strengthen your communication, your brand and your message, OR it can weaken it.

You're always communicating something, even when you say nothing. You're always informing people of your worth, even when you sit at the back and never speak.

How do you hold yourself? How do you enter a room? Do you stare downward, avoiding eye contact with people?

Is your body language uncomfortable, awkward, and tentative? Do you look unsure of yourself?

Is your body language silly and amateurish? Or do you look like a leader and project confidence?

How you present yourself will change how people perceive you. It may not be fair to judge someone by how they look, but it's reality and we're all guilty of it all the time.

TIPS

- *Always dress for the position you want, not the position you're in.* When I was a teaching assistant, I always got mistaken for a professor because I looked the part.
- *Practice!* —You must practice making an entrance, looking people in the eye when you introduce yourself, delivering a confident handshake. *You don't just learn this stuff through osmosis. You must practice and train and ask for feedback.*
- *Assess your wardrobe.* Invest in key pieces that make you feel confident and look like a superstar! Know how to dress for your body type and size. Have a signature look that makes you stand out from the crowd. My signature look is my red hair, bold lip color and statement necklace. I also love booties!!!!
- *Record yourself talking.* Analyze your body language. Look at your posture and hand or arm movements. Listen to the tone and pitch of your voice. Do you drone on or sound enthusiastic? Ask others to provide feedback.
- *Join a social club!* At the ALL IN club we conduct public speaking drills for 90 minutes. Everyone talks and then receives immediate feedback on what they did well and what they need to work on. Join a club that forces you to speak aloud and practice your communication skills.

Do You Know How to Sit in a Chair?

I notice this problem in conferences, meetings and even in my own classroom. There is a distinct difference between how men and women sit in chairs. It seems so simple it's almost comical. Do I really need to write about "how to sit in a chair"? —Well, read on, my friend, read on, and see if you've ever sat like this in a chair.

How you sit in a chair speaks to your confidence level. It tells others how seriously to take you.

Women take up the least amount of space in a chair; they tend to crawl into the sides or back in a huddled, passive position.

Women would share a seat with someone else if asked. I'm sure some women would even sit on the floor if asked. You think I'm kidding? Sadly, I'm not.

Two semesters ago during my lecture for 180 students in a room that only seated 180, there would always be latecomers who would SIT ON THE FLOOR (they were always women, no joke), instead of walking down the stairs to the first few rows and taking a seat.

There are women who prefer to stand for a full two-hour lecture than have to "interrupt" a row of students to find a seat.

One young woman told me she would rather skip my lecture than arrive late and have the "whole class look at her" as she opened the door and looked around for a seat!!

Here's a picture of how much space a man typically takes up in a chair. See? They take up the WHOLE chair. Leaning forward, looking confident, even when they don't know squat!

Compare that to how a woman typically sits in a chair. See how women take up less room? So prim and proper—sitting on half-a-chair.

TIPS ON HOW TO SIT[66]

- *Where do you sit?* Most importantly, take a seat at the table! Not at the back of the room, not at the side of the room against the wall, but at the actual table where the decision-makers sit.

- *What does your posture look like in a chair?* You want both feet firmly planted on the ground. You want to be leaning forward slightly. Don't slouch. You can cross your legs, but if you're making an important point, I still think you need to have both feet on the ground. *Sit like a Yogi.* Ever notice the beautiful posture of dancers or serious Yoga practitioners? Stunning. Sit like them. And do NOT sit on your legs curled under you. I actually see

this quite often in meetings. It's gross and it looks like you're on a picnic. Never take your shoes off, ever. Ever. There's nothing more déclassé than a woman kicking off her shoes in the summer, only to make everyone else breathe in the glory of smelly summer feet. So unprofessional.

- *Where are your hands when seated?* Put your hands on the table. Seriously. Don't cross your arms, don't have clenched fists. Don't fiddle with things. Don't sit on your hands. Bring them up on the table.

- *Where do you look when seated?* Make eye contact. Look directly at the speaker with a soft smile. I have to remind myself to smile otherwise my natural resting facial expression looks slightly bitchy. No joke.

- *What to bring? (Travel lightly!)* You don't need to bring your lunch, a snack, a 2L bottle of water, breath mints, a calculator and a pack of pens to a meeting. A notepad, a pen and one H_2O bottle should suffice. Anything more looks cluttered and disorganized.

How to Give a Proper Handshake

Doesn't shaking someone's hand seem so basic? Like, who doesn't know how to shake a hand properly? —Well, most women, actually. Do you know how women typically shake hands? It's the dreaded limp handshake. You know—the one that just sort of sits in your hand with no strength or confidence to it. It actually almost feels like an apology.

First impressions matter and if you're offering a limp handshake, it means you're not confident and even you don't believe in your abilities. So why should anyone else (especially someone looking to hire you)?

The handshake speaks volumes about you without you even uttering a single word. Obviously, you don't want to seem like a wrestler when you're shaking their hand, but your handshake should give the impression that you're serious, you know what you're talking about and you're confident!

Bad handshakes are hard to forget. Ever get your hand crushed by someone? It friggin' hurts! I've actually had instances where I said "ouch" after someone shook my hand. I've also been grossed out by how wet, clammy and sweaty someone's hand is.

A 2001 study done by psychologist Dr. William Chaplin revealed that extroverts are more likely to offer a firm handshake and introverts are more likely to offer a limp handshake.[67] Guess which handshake made a better first impression?

Most people don't realize how important the handshake is. You will shake a lot of hands throughout your career and networking opportunities, so you better learn how to do it properly.

TIPS

- *Make sure your hands are dry.* If you have sweaty hands, then carry Kleenex or a handkerchief with you. If all else fails, dry your hands on the side of your pants before shaking hands.
- *If someone doesn't offer their hand to you first, then reach forward and offer yours.* It's a sign of confidence. No one will leave you hanging.
- *Always maintain eye contact.* Don't look around the room to see if there's anyone more important to talk to.
- *Offer a firm grip.* But don't try to dominate them with an excessively forceful grip.
- *Say "Nice to meet you, my name is —." Smile. Let the handshake go.* Just like that.

Now practice this with friends or family (both men and women). Ask for feedback.

Body Language: Do's and Don'ts

- *Don't slouch!* Stand tall, stand proud. Good posture projects confidence. Slouching makes you look unsure of yourself and by extension the material you're presenting. You shouldn't cross your ankles, cross your arms, lean forward on one arm, or hang on to the podium.

- *Stop touching your hair.* It's gross. Usually only women do this. It looks unprofessional and it's annoying. I once counted how many times a female speaker touched her hair during her speech, and after 27 times I stopped counting. I had also stopped listening. I just didn't take her seriously anymore.

- *Don't clench your fists.* It makes you look nervous, and then the audience gets nervous, because they're wondering what the heck is wrong with you. Are you pissed off? Are you about to punch the podium? It also makes you look STRESSED OUT. All of which is not conducive to a relaxed atmosphere. And don't clench the podium tightly. It's not going anywhere.

- *Stop rattling the change in your pocket.* Men do this all the time, and it's noisy and distracting. Also, why do you have all that change in your pocket? Who carries change anymore?

- *Do not sniffle!* If you have a stuffed-up nose or sinus issues, use a tissue, but do NOT sniffle. Super-annoying and makes you look unkempt. Blow your nose before you speak, have a box of Kleenex beside you, and after your talk use some hand sanitizer. You'll usually have questions after your talk or people wanting to meet you, and if they've seen you touch your nose, all they're thinking about now is the germs on your hands.

- *Don't play with your pen or papers.* If you can't handle having a pen beside you while you speak because you'll play with it and move it around, making noises, then don't have a pen there. Simple! Also, do not rattle your papers. And don't tap your fingers on the podium. It makes it seem as if you're pressed for time and in a hurry to leave. Did you double-book yourself or something?

- *Make eye contact.* Who are you speaking to? I've listened to speakers who never made eye contact with anyone in the room. It's the most bizarre feeling. I actually just had a guest lecturer come in and she spoke to the side-walls, the back door, the clock, her notes, the teleprompter, the projection screen, but never to anyone in the room!! Weird, right? All the students commented on it. But, it was just nerves on her part. One quick trick I've used over 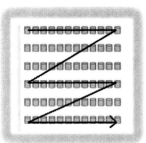 the years is to make a mental box in my mind, and then I start speaking in a zigzag manner. I'll speak to the back left row first, then jump to the back right row, then move to the middle left, than top right and so on and so on. Or you can think about drawing an "X" in your mind and speaking to each quadrant (top-left, bottom-right, bottom-left, top-right).

- *Do not, under any circumstances, apologize.* Hey, ladies! Do you hear me? Do NOT apologize. Don't apologize for the projection screen breaking down, don't apologize if you've lost your place in your notes, or if your notes are out of order. (Hint: Don't have your notes out of order!) Don't apologize if you're nervous, and for the love of God (I'd like to think She watches out for nervous speakers) do not say "Oh, I'm so nervous speaking in public," or "I'm not the best speaker, so bear with me" or "I hope you'll be a good audience, because this is my first speech ever." Ahhhhhhhhhh. Why would you say those things? Have you ever in your life heard a man say that? When in doubt, state the facts, take emotion out of it, and never, ever apologize.

- *Don't turn your back to the audience.* Oh. My. Goodness. Have you ever listened to a speaker who reads the PowerPoint slides with their back to the audience? This happens all the time and it's horrible. I've asked speakers to move away from the projection screen because I can't see the slides, and I've also had to ask speakers to TURN AROUND because it's hard to hear them when they've got their back to the audience. Remember: You're speaking to the audience, not the wall. Speak directly to them, engage them, and keep their attention. That's your job.

- *Go easy on the hand gestures.* Are you ground crew, guiding planes to their proper gates at the airport? Are you a cop, directing traffic at an intersection because the stoplight is out? If not, what the heck are you doing with your arms? Now, hand gestures when used appropriately can add dynamism to your speech, but taken to the extreme they make you look scattered. Don't make sharp chopping gestures, unless you're an Iron Chef contestant. Don't swing your hands widely from left to right, and don't keep repeating the same gesture.

- *No noisy jewelry.* I love jewelry! Wow, do I love a good statement necklace or chunky watch or sparkly bracelets! But if your audience can HEAR your jewelry, then you've got a problem. I figured this one out while supervising an exam for my students. I thought I had a terrific outfit on, and then, as I was answering their exam questions, I realized my bracelets were banging together and disturbing the entire room. Jewelry is meant to be seen and admired, but not heard.

- *Smile!* Please. You need to smile, especially at the beginning. Don't ever start a speech without looking directly at the audience and smiling. It just sets the right tone. Now, you may not want to do this if you're giving a eulogy, but for anything non-death-related, smile. It's the first impression the audience has of you.

- *Stop fidgeting.* Don't fidget with your clothes, hair, jewelry, papers, glasses, water bottle, microphone, etc. Don't keep clearing your throat. If you need a sip of water, drink some. I once listened to a female presenter who adjusted and re-adjusted the scarf she was wearing so many times I started wondering where she had got it, because I liked it. Then I started thinking about shopping, making a list of errands I needed to run after work, and guess what? I completely stopped listening to the speaker. Fidgeting can distract your audience and once you've lost an audience, it's difficult to get them back.

Phew! That's all for now.

I didn't get there
by wishing for it
or hoping for it,
BUT by working
for it.

—*Estée Lauder,*
cosmetics titan

5

Self-
Promotion

The Importance of Self-Promotion

Women are embarrassed by self-promotion, while men do it instinctively or intuitively. You must be your own advocate, you must sell yourself, your talents, brand and experience, because NO ONE else will do this for you.

Women wait to be noticed because they assume everyone is playing by the same rules, while men demand attention by bending the rules to their advantage.

For some odd reason, women have completely internalized the belief that if we do good work, someone, somewhere will notice us. This is crazy.

You can bet you will NOT get what you don't ask for.

Linda Babcock co-wrote a book called *Women Don't Ask*,[68] where she makes the point that *"women ask for raises and promotions 85% less often than men, and women ask for 30% less than their male counterparts when asking for a raise."*[69]

This is insanity! So WHY does it happen?—Because women don't recognize opportunities. They wait for them. Men create them.

Opportunities are everywhere, except that they're masked as hurdles, barriers, obstacles, problems and complaints.

We think our situation or the rules are fixed and rigid when in reality everything is fluid, everything is changeable—even the rules.

We're taught to just "be grateful," to "be happy with what you have." When we ask for more, others tell us, "Don't be greedy. They could rescind the offer." Worst of all, we HESITATE at the worst moment. This hesitation to ask for more, self-promote or negotiate affects our confidence and our paychecks. While we're hesitating, men have what researchers call *"honest over-confidence."* That's a natural overestimation of their abilities. In fact, men rate their performance as 30% better than it actually is.[70] As women, we need a little bit of that "honest over-confidence" ourselves.

Ladies, listen to me!

1. Promote yourselves.
2. Recognize that opportunities are everywhere.
3. Learn from successful people, and stop listening to those who haven't achieved success. Stop taking advice from people who fear taking risks and constantly doubt themselves.

Successful people promote, others wait around for a promotion.

Self-Promotion Techniques

Self-promotion shouldn't be a dirty word. It shouldn't make you cringe or develop uncontrollable anxiety.

Self-promotion is the key to success, because if people don't know what you do, what services you provide, what skills you have or what products you sell, then you're NOWHERE.

Get out of obscurity. Get into the limelight.

If you're not visible, your business, brand or idea will tank. It will never prosper.

If you're not promoting yourself and your ideas, then you're promoting someone else's vision.

Be prepared to promote your idea, your skills and your experience anywhere and at any time.

When you're in line at Starbucks and someone asks what you do for a living, can you pitch them your brand or your company in 30 seconds or less?

Always be prepared to deliver a pitch to anyone in any environment. Always back up your pitch with evidence, a story or a memorable statistic.

Always ask for the sale. What do you want from the other person? Ask for their time, ask for an opportunity to discuss your ideas further, ask for something.

Always get the other person's contact information. Forget about handing out your business cards, they're going in the garbage as soon as you turn your back. Get their contact information and then email them immediately. I mean, as soon as you walk away, take out your phone and email them. This will distinguish you from everyone else who will wait a "polite" amount of time to establish contact.

Develop a pitch that's so natural, so passionate, so enthusiastic that your energy is contagious and people just "naturally" want to know more. For example, while standing in line for my iced Americano at Starbucks, I say: "Did you know that men negotiate four times as often as women, and when women actually do negotiate, they end up asking for 30% less than men? Isn't that crazy?" And every single time I've said this, the other person says something like: "Yup, I can believe that. I've made that mistake myself. . . . I hate negotiating. . . . My friend just signed a contract without negotiating." Then they immediately ask, "How did you know that? What do you do?" Bam! Perfect opportunity to get into my research, the book, my blog, my social club. I've got their attention, I hooked them with an interesting statistic, we've bonded over a shared experience and now I'll ASK FOR THE SALE. I'll ask them to check out my blog or buy my book.

Pitch, promote, discuss. These should all become a natural extension of who you are.

Promote to everyone, everywhere and at all times. Everyone is a potential client.

A personal example: To promote this book I take it everywhere with me. I casually bring it up in EVERY conversation I have, whether that be at my local Starbucks, the grocery store, my daughter's daycare or when I run into my former students at the mall. It's as simple as answering the question "Hi Maja, what's new?" I respond: "Great! My first book just got published!" Then I pull out the book and start talking about it. I've practiced condensing the book's message into a 30-second pitch and then I talk about it everywhere I go. If you're proud of what you do and passionate about it, you *want* to share the news. It's not really about "selling," it's about sharing. I'm in the zone, I'm enthusiastic and I just want others to know this information.

Promote yourself at work by taking every opportunity to showcase your RESULTS and accomplishments. Just remember to organize your skills, talents and experiences around the VALUE you ADD to the company. It's about blending your unique talents and pitching them as invaluable to your boss, your new client or job prospects.

It's about your skills PLUS the value you add. That's the synergistic power of promotion!

Instead of viewing self-promotion as boastful and pushy, start seeing it as a way for you to develop some swagger! Self-promotion is self-pride.

I'm so tired of blogs and articles telling people to stop self-promotion. Women have kept their opinions to themselves long enough. *We've kept our heads down; we didn't interrupt for fear of being rude; we sat on the sidelines and cheered on others; we silenced ourselves out of fear and kept our skills and talents to ourselves. Where did that get us?*

Nowhere! That's why we have so few female leaders, CEOs, CFOs, and heads of state.

Stop this nonsense.

Self-promote and don't look back.

TIPS

- *Keep an updated list of your achievements in your wallet.* Just as you should be updating your CV or resume on a regular basis, you need to have a list of your talents, accomplishments, experiences and skills on hand at all times. Refer to this list daily. Memorize it, internalize it and believe in it.

- *Practice!* Don't assume you can ad lib and sound articulate and thoughtful. You can't. Most people can't. Ever listen to a wedding speech or an impromptu toast? Ninety-nine percent are embarrassing. Practice your pitch at home. Record yourself, analyze yourself, ask for feedback and then revise and practice again.

What Are You Selling?

Everyone is a salesperson, whether you believe it or not. I know that "teacher" or "designer" may sound better than "salesperson," but selling—the act of selling—is a part of every single job, career or profession. And the sooner you get comfortable with selling, the sooner you can finally start achieving your dreams.[71]

Selling is the art of persuading or influencing people to go along with your way, to buy into your ideas.

Are you a student trying to get into graduate school? Then you need to "sell" the graduate admissions committee on why you're the right candidate.

Are you applying for a new job? Then you need to sell the interviewer, HR manager or company that you're the perfect person for the job. You need to stand out from the 200 other resumes lying in a pile.

Are you starting a new business? Then you need to "sell" the bank on your astute business plan, in order to get adequate funding.

Are you a designer, yoga studio owner, blogger or creative person? Then you need clients! You need revenue; you need people to buy into your idea, your product or services. Therefore, you need to sell your brand to others, so that they shop with you and not the competition.

Selling is involved in every single transaction, communication, debate or exchange of ideas.

If you're not selling something to someone, then you're being sold something. It's "sell or be sold," as master salesman Grant Cardone puts it.[72]

Ever get up-sold a pastry to go with your latté at Starbucks? You got sold!

Ever purchase a lipstick, jacket or that perfect little black dress even when you had absolutely NO intention of buying that day? You got sold.

But it didn't feel bad, did it? That's the same reciprocal feeling you want to create in your daily interactions with people.

Selling has to be a two-way street. It can't be a win-lose situation, or you'll never go back to that store or salesperson again. But if you left the store feeling good about the sale, even though you weren't going to buy that day, then it was a win-win situation.

Remember, if you're not selling the brilliance of your ideas, products or services to other people, then you're being sold someone else's dream. If you're not working on achieving your dreams, then you're working on someone else's.

It's not that complicated. I sell everywhere I go, to anyone I meet, because I'm proud of what I do. I believe so wholeheartedly in my product and message of female empowerment that it doesn't really feel like "selling." It just feels like getting people on board. I want to share my enthusiasm and get more women leaning into their careers and aware of their self-sabotaging habits.

Let Aliza Licht, SVP of global communications at Donna Karen International, explain it: "You need to think like a publicist. But a publicist for yourself. You are the brand."[73]

Start Speaking in Sound Bites

Successful people get right to the point. They don't bore you with endless details and confuse you with rhetoric. The next time you have a networking opportunity, run into someone who could potentially hire you, or speak to someone you admire—what will you say?

When you ask most graduate students what their thesis is about, they go ON, and ON, and ON. Five minutes later, you're bored out of your mind and have absolutely no idea what they're talking about. Then you start wondering if this person will ever shut up and how they'll get a job in the real world, when even the response to a simple question ("What are you studying?") turns into a 2,000-word monologue.

One of my undergraduate mentors told me that any graduate student should be able to explain their thesis in 30 words and in less than one minute. If you can't do that, you're not ready to begin your research yet.

This is so true! We need to take this advice and apply it to other realms in our lives.

Picture this: You're at a conference and you run into your academic idol (is this a thing?!). You have ONE MINUTE to talk to them because there's a line-up of 30 other students wishing to make a good impression. What will you say?

"Blah, blah, blah, blah, mumble, mumble, indecipherable nonsense." Silence. Then smile weirdly at them and pray they ask you to be part of their new research team. And your moment is over. NEXT person, please!

See what I mean? This happens all the time. You need to prepare for these chance meetings and networking opportunities. Prepare to impress.

You need to be succinct, to the point and memorable.

Who are you and what do you do?

And the most crucial question of all: *WHAT VALUE DO YOU BRING?* Why is what you do so important? What gap does it fill in the world? Why are you the person to do it?

To answer these questions you must speak in sound bites and tag lines. Every great company has a memorable tag line.

Nike: "Just Do It."

American Express: "Don't Leave Home Without It."

MasterCard: "There Are Some Things Money Can't Buy. For Everything Else, There's MasterCard."

L'Oréal: "Because You're Worth It."

Now you need to develop one for yourself. Practice! Write out a few tag lines, say them aloud, say them to other people as you shake their hands and see if they sound natural and confident.

For instance: "My name is Professor Maja. I'm the founder of ALL IN. I help women turn fear into success."

Then be quiet. Wait for the other person to say hello. Inevitably they'll ask, "What's ALL IN about?" or "Tell me a little more about that."

Then you go into your two-minute elevator pitch. For example:

First, I explain the problem: "Women aren't going ALL IN with their education and careers. There's a lack of female leaders. *Then I explain how I fill the gap:* "I conduct workshops and seminars for women in all areas of life (high school, college, university, starting out their careers), and I provide them with strategies and tools to fulfill their potential by teaching them to be more effective communicators."

When they like what they've heard, they'll ask you questions and a natural conversation will occur.

At the end of the "meeting" you must ASK FOR THE SALE. You must close the conversation by asking for something. What do you want? A job? A paid job or a volunteer gig? Do you want to learn more from this person? Do you need a 15-minute coffee meeting with them? Do you need their opinion on something? Well, then, ASK!

Never leave a networking opportunity without asking for the sale. For example, after I've met someone new and spoken about my business or my book, I'll say, "Why don't you check out my blog?" or "Why don't you join me for some public speaking drills at my social club, it's free to join" or "Check out my book on Amazon, I think you'll really like it."

Look for Opportunities to Speak

Public speaking isn't a skill that you can develop without practice. So practice! Look for any and all opportunities to speak in public, in formal and informal settings. There are two ways to improve your public speaking skills: (1) through intentional and deliberate practice; and (2) by employing constant assessment and feedback.

Can you make a toast? I was once asked to fill in as emcee for a wedding with less than 24 hours' notice. Terrifying! But I did it and when my jokes fell flat and there was total silence in a room full of 250 people—yup. I. Freaked. Out. (On the inside.) On the outside, I calmly asked the audience if my microphone was turned on, because I thought that would get a few chuckles for sure. Nothing. Nada. But, after 30 minutes of winging it, I found my stride and my jokes started landing and my ad-libbing was awesome.

How can you practice your public speaking?

- Prepare a five-minute speech that you'll deliver without notes. Videotape yourself and then ask for feedback. Identify your speaking habits (e.g., nervous tics, overuse of filler words, awkward body language).
- Join the debate team on campus.
- Join a public speaking club like Toastmasters.
- Start or join a book club.
- Practice rapid-fire-style debates: Pick a random topic and speak about it for 30 seconds to your friends. Take turns giving constructive feedback to each other.
- Raise your hand in class more often and ask questions.
- Speak up in meetings at work.
- Ask your boss for more challenging assignments, perhaps ones that put you in a position where you have to lead a team project.

- If your food isn't to your liking at a restaurant, speak with the waiter and send it back. (So often women refuse to send back a meal because they're worried about offending the waiter or the cook, they don't want to make a scene, or it just makes them uncomfortable.) Force yourself to speak up next time your meal isn't good.
- Conduct mock interviews with your family and friends, where you practice answering the most common interview questions.
- Watch the experts! —Watch TED Talks like Amy Cuddy's "Your Body Language Shapes Who You Are" and leadership coach Olivia Fox Cabane's "Build Your Personal Charisma" as examples of confident women speakers.

The one thing you can count on is that if you don't practice your public speaking, you will not get better! It's that simple.

Don't wait around for other people to be happy for you. Any happiness you get you've got to make yourself.

—*Alice Walker, writer, poet and activist*

6

Career Strategies

Use Technology or Get Used by It

I got totally used by technology. It was a cerebral assault. And I didn't even mind.

Then I started hanging out with successful people. I made note of their schedules and I realized that really successful people don't watch TV. They only use Instagram to post images of their own success. They only tweet out information related to their own business, ideas or brands.

Ah, where have I been? On a Netflix bender of three seasons of *House of Cards*, five seasons of *Downton Abbey* and the first season of *Orange Is the New Black*. Down the rabbit hole of Pinterest looking at gourmet vegan food so opulent and decadently prepared that I knew I'd never attempt the recipes, but I wanted to feel like a chef so I browsed for another 30 minutes.

Then when I want to feel like I'm living in *Architectural Digest* I spend time browsing the decorating site Houzz. You should see how utterly gorgeous my house is in my dreams. I mean *stunning*.

All of my students complain about procrastination while simultaneously admitting how much time they waste on Netflix, Facebook, Instagram, Pinterest and Twitter.

Kim Kardashian in her latest interview was asked what shows she likes to watch. Her answer: She doesn't have time to watch TV! —She's the biggest reality television star and she doesn't watch TV. OK. Holy crap, lesson learned for me!

Steve Jobs limited the use of technology in his home. You'd think his kids would have had iPads in every room, but he didn't allow it. He wanted to foster creativity in his kids.

Every technology titan LIMITS THE AMOUNT OF TECHNOLOGY they and their families use. *What?*[74]

Why did no one tell me this?

I listened to a comedian complain that he was "done with Netflix, meaning I'm literally done watching everything on Netflix," and I had to laugh—and then cry a little—at how true this was.

I had to quit using technology for entertainment. I hadn't had cable in more than 10 years, so I felt a little boastful at my productivity, but then I started actually ADDING UP THE HOURS I spent online and it was a little distressing. Ever spend an hour watching something on YouTube and then realize the time you've wasted? Like "I can NOT believe I just spent an hour watching T.V. news bloopers!"

TIP

- Cut yourself off from one pitiful website or TV show at a time. No more Facebook updates until the end of the day. No more browsing Pinterest or Instagram if you haven't accomplished your priority list and pushed yourself and your career forward.

Email Etiquette

Please follow these guidelines to ensure your emails reflect you in the best possible manner.

1. *Add the email address LAST.* Write your email first, and then type in the recipient's email. This ensures you'll never accidentally hit SEND before your email is ready.

2. *Use an appropriate greeting.* "Hi/Hello is always appropriate, or "Good morning/afternoon." You must include a greeting, even if it's just "Hello." Don't use casual language like "Hey," "What's up," or "Yo".

3. *Include a signoff.* Always end with your name, or consider including a signature line and a signoff such as "Regards," "Thanks" or "Best wishes," "Sincerely," or "Best."

4. *Use a professional email address.* No one will open an email from toocool69@hotmail.com. If you want to be taken seriously, have a professional email address that includes your name in it. Otherwise, it's going into spam.

5. *Subject line must be concise.* A simple subject line is like a summary of your email. Being concise helps filter messages and prevents them from being spammed.

6. *Assess the tone.* Never send emails when you're upset or angry. Hostility and sarcasm are easy to spot, so always make sure your emails are professional in tone. Whatever you send by email, think about whether you would feel comfortable saying it face-to-face. Your emails should always be respectful and approachable in tone.

7. *Proofread your email before you send it.* Your emails create an impression. Before you hit send, ensure the email corresponds to the best version of yourself. Every single interaction with people is an opportunity to present yourself in either a positive or negative manner. Make sure your spelling, grammar and sentence structure are accurate throughout.

8. *Format your emails.* It's helpful to break your emails up into separate paragraphs, with lots of space. Use bullets or number your points. It easier and faster to read that way.

9. *Never use lowercase "i."* It is never appropriate to write the first-person singular pronoun ("I") in lowercase ("i"). It must be capitalized. OH MY GOODNESS, so many students make this mistake. Don't be one of them. It looks sloppy and unprofessional.

10. *Avoid texting lingo in professional emails.* Texting lingo such as TTYL, thx, LOL, b4, btw, l8r, cya (or any other texting abbreviation) should be avoided. It just doesn't look professional.

11. *Limit emoticons!* Holy crap, is this ever unprofessional! Use emoticons with your friends and family, and not in professional emails. If you feel comfortable and know the person well enough, OR if they've already used them, then use them sparingly. If your email reads harshly and you need to use a smiley face to make it seem softer, reconsider your choice of words.

12. *Spell people's names correctly.* It's just rude to misspell the name of the person you're emailing; especially since this information is readily available. People frequently misspell my name and use "y" instead of a "j". It may seem inconsequential but it's not. It's about respect.

13. *Always respond to all emails.* Even if you received a message in error, reply back, "Oops, I think you meant to send this to someone else." It takes a minute and it's polite. If you need more time before answering back, send an email that says "I got your message; I'm tied up now, but will respond by end of day." I've actually NOT hired people based on their email response time. One research candidate took over two full days to respond to an email, while the other three candidates responded within an hour. Everyone has a smart phone, so there's no excuse for tardy email response times.

14. *Don't send unexpected attachments.* Always acknowledge that you've attached a document. Make sure your files are appropriately named like "ResumeSmith2015.doc", rather than "File00276.doc".

15. *Only copy people if absolutely necessary.* Use CC sparingly and copy people on your email only if they absolutely need to be involved.

16. *Beware of* REPLY ALL. Everyone hates reading email chains from 10 people. Learn how to distinguish between REPLY and REPLY ALL or risk looking really foolish.

17. *Don't write a novel!* Everyone is pressed for time. Get to the point. Be concise! Do not write several paragraphs when usually one or two sentences will suffice. Be considerate of people's time, including your own. If you have to write a lot, add some space. It's easier to read.

18. *Remember, nothing is private anymore.* Emails should not be considered private, because they're not. Your email account is the property of your work/university, so make sure whatever you write in your emails doesn't embarrass you or the company you work for.

19. *Assume the best.* If you get a curt reply, don't internalize it. Assessing the correct tone in emails is difficult. People are busy! *I can't emphasize this enough.* Everyone is trying to get as much done in as little time as possible, so don't over think a brisk response. I once had a professor who only responded in 10 words or less. That was his rule. At first I was offended, but then I saw how much he got done in a day, and I realized that was just his time management plan.

20. *Never send chain emails.* This should be a no-brainer, but it isn't. So: *Never send chain emails in a professional setting.* I hate getting them from friends or family, let alone at work.

Social Media Mistakes

The very first thing employers do when selecting candidates for a job interview is to Google them. You can count on it. Potential employers will look through your Facebook page, your Twitter feed, and your LinkedIn account. They'll look at your Instagram pictures and your Pinterest board. They'll read your website or blogs, and they'll watch your videos on YouTube or Vimeo if you have them. Employers expect you to have a life outside of work, but what they don't want to see are:

- Embarrassing or sexy photos of you;
- Anything alcohol- or drug-related;
- Anything illegal; or
- Anything racist, homophobic or insensitive.

Using social media means . . .	Getting used by social media means . . .
• You're generating interest, networking opportunities and new experiences. • People are impressed with your social media presence. • You're getting new business, new clients and new revenue through your sites. • You're learning something new through social media.	• There's no career, social or financial benefit for you. • You waste your time reading about what people ate or watching cute animal videos. • You don't learn anything on other people's social media, and no one learns anything of value by logging onto your sites either. • Social media distracts you from your career goals.

Use social media to further your career, don't get used by it.
Across all your social media sites there must be CON-SISTENCY. Who are you and what are you about? This should be

clear from all your sites. So your bio, photo, tag line or brand message should be consistent.

Google yourself and see what you find. Then you know what you need to fix.

Edit, hide or delete discriminating photos. Yes, you won that wet T-shirt contest, but employers don't need to see your T & A shots. OK? So, remove or hide ALL photos of you holding (or being around) alcohol, weed or any other drug. Don't look drunk in photos—not cool. Get rid of any booty shots or "sexy selfies." Delete, delete, delete. Be proud of every photo you're in. If you wouldn't feel comfortable showing your employer a photo, don't post it.

Make sure all your social media sites are up-to-date. Update profiles, CV's, resumes, email addresses and Twitter handles.

Include a photo (normally a head shot). Everyone likes to know what you look like so they can put a picture to a name.

Include a creative tagline, so it's immediately clear what you're interested in and what your goals and vision are.

Remember, nothing is private on your social media site. People can take your photos and change them, alter them or use them in ways that you didn't expect.

Artist Richard Price has taken people's Instagram screen shots and edited them to include comments he made. He then sold these photos. There's no copyright infringement because he technically "altered" them, so his actions are considered fair use for artistic purposes.[75] Remember this the next time you're itching to boast about your weekend or beer counts or shopping sprees.

Learn How to Network

As a newly graduated Ph.D., I went to a few networking lunches and was overwhelmed with undergraduates and Master's students giving me their business cards just because I had graduated. At the end of one lunch I had 13 business cards and I didn't know who any of them were.

I tossed the cards out and went to another networking meeting. There I saw the same thing occur, except this time it was Ph.D.'s inundating the post-doctoral students and newly hired professors with cards. I asked one professor what he did with all the business cards. He discreetly put a napkin over them and slid them into the wastebasket. That's the hard truth.

Networking works both ways. There must be a benefit to both parties, otherwise what's the point?

You must learn to get comfortable with networking, and do it in a new way.[76]

First, *find common ground!* When you're seated next to someone at a dinner, conference or meeting, take the opportunity to get to know them. Ask them about their work and what they are passionate about. Try to find a connection. Don't start every encounter with the attitude of "What can this person do for me?" People see right through that. I've been in the middle of conversations with people when their eyes darted around, looking for a better, more successful person to speak with. It doesn't feel good, so don't do it to others.

Stay in touch! You must feed your networking contacts. You don't need to talk to them weekly, but don't let a whole year go by either. Feed them and they'll grow (sounds like you're planting tomatoes or something, but it's true, I swear!). If you don't keep the conversation going with your contacts, they'll cease to be of any use.

Diversify! You need a diverse group of networking contacts. Look to grow your contacts and friendships beyond your own business or academic circles. You need people in different sectors with different opinions that can help provide you with feedback or advice when needed.

Reciprocate! If you see something of value for one of your contacts, pass it along. It's that simple. A quick email, tweet or text ("I saw this and thought it might be of some use for you"). When someone sends something of value my way, I always respond with a polite "thank you." That's how you keep your network alive.

Reach out to people you admire. Just because you don't know someone doesn't mean you can't congratulate them on their latest success, or tell them how much you enjoyed their book/blog/artwork/article, etc. It's great if they respond, but sometimes they won't. That's OK. You were sharing your enthusiasm for their work. Keep doing this.

Socialize with different people. Force yourself to attend out-of-your-comfort-zone functions. Get to know a wide variety of people: artists, musicians, philanthropists, economists, educators, businesspeople, entrepreneurs, etc. Go to art exhibits, book signings, parties, and more. This is WAY easier said than done, I know, because I struggle with it, too. Some of my role models and mentors make sure they socialize twice a week. I can't handle that frequency, so I'm aiming for once or twice a month. But I have to remind myself and schedule it into my calendar, otherwise I won't do it. Socializing more often with diverse groups of people and businesses serves three main purposes:

1. It helps you grow your network.
2. You learn from others. You need to know what's happening in other sectors of life, who's working on cutting-edge stuff, who has a new book out, what's the new way of thinking about an issue.
3. It forces you to self-promote! Everyone should know what you do for a living, what services you provide or products you sell. The next time someone needs a research assistant,

will they think of you? The next time someone needs consulting work done, will they think of you? —That's what you want to happen. Learn about others, and make sure they learn about you and your skills.

Finally, *send a note!* If you've had a memorable conversation with someone at a conference, meeting, or in a chance encounter, then maximize the moment by sending them a note saying how nice it was to meet and how much you enjoyed speaking. Make the extra effort, because most people won't, and it's an easy way to stand out in the sea of mediocrity.[77]

Finding a Mentor

First rule of finding a mentor: don't ask someone to mentor you. It's cringe-worthy. Worse yet is that no one tells you these things.

What I've learned during my years in academia is that it comes down to your performance and potential.

Mentorships happen copacetically; they cannot be forced. They occur when a mentor sees potential in someone and offers something of value to further encourage that growth. This connection between the two people is reciprocal, and when done correctly both benefit. No one wants to mentor someone they don't get along with.

> If you are successful, it is because somewhere, sometime, someone gave you a life or an idea that started you in the right direction. Remember also that you are indebted to life until you help some less fortunate person, just as you were helped.
> —*Melinda Gates, activist, philanthropist*

How do you find a mentor? First thing you need to do is catch their attention in a good way. Become familiar to this person. Work with them, for them, alongside them or volunteer for them. If you don't know them yet, you need to pitch them with those 30-second, one-minute, or two-minute elevator pitches that you've practiced with military precision. You better be prepared! Take advantage of every chance meeting in the hallway, coffee shop or parking lot. These are brief but essential moments for you to push through the crowd and stand out. Have something meaningful to say and be prepared to execute your pitch at a moment's notice.

A great mentor will push you past your comfort zone. Mentors believe in your capabilities but won't take any crap from you either. They'll force you to start taking ownership for your career and your success, and encourage you to do things you never thought possible. Great mentors have been fundamental to where I am today and have encouraged me every step of the way before, during, and beyond my Ph.D.

This is how a real mentorship should develop. I'm currently mentoring some young women. They never asked me to mentor them; it happened organically as I got to know them over several of my courses and saw their work ethic, determination, and positive attitude. If you're not a go-getter, no one's getting you. Get it?

Look for like-minded peers and mentor each other. Don't discount the value that peers can provide. Support, validation, and encouragement from people who (like yourself) are fiercely going after their goals is a gift. Harness that positive energy.

A mentorship is a professional relationship. Friendships may develop over time, but never forget this is professional. Take it seriously. Nobody wants to hand-hold you, so maximize your opportunities. Learn everything you can. Then pay it forward when it's your turn.

My own mentor experience: After I did a presentation in one of my undergrad sociology courses, my professor, Dr. Lorne Tepperman, pulled me aside after class and told me how articulate and confident I sounded when I spoke. He asked me if I'd be interested in being part of his work-study team. I distinctly remember feeling super-special and immediately called my mom to tell her that my sociology professor "thinks I'm smart enough to be on his team!" Fast forward 12+ years and he's still mentoring me. I've worked on every major research project he's had and his recommendations have turned into dozens of other opportunities for me. And each and every time I work for him I give him 150%. I don't ask for overtime, I just do the work and do it spectacularly well. And now I pay it forward, by mentoring young women myself.

You Only Need One Supporter
. . . For Now

Sometimes when you're trying something new or you're going against the "norm," people really resist. They give you a hard time, they don't support you or, even worse, they openly discourage you. Please don't be disheartened when your failures bring others joy. This will happen. Just remember that all you need for now is ONE supporter. And if you don't have one, let me be the first. I support you.

No one is going to ever be as passionate about your dreams as you are. That's the truth. And that's OK. Oh my goodness, can I tell you a story? When the first draft of this book came out, I proudly showed it off to a work colleague. "Look!!! It's my first book. I just picked it up today from the publisher!!" And her response: "Oh . . . cool." THAT'S IT!!!! Two words, that's all she could muster up. Then she proceeded to look through the menu for lunch. She didn't ask me ONE question, not one. Like, "What's your book about?" or "How long did it take to write it?" OR "Congratulations!" Nothing. It was such a debilitating experience that I unfortunately let it affect me for the rest of the day. Her reaction just totally bummed me out. Then I had to remind myself that *no one is going to ever be as passionate about your dreams as you are.* Sad, but oh so true.

As long as you have ONE supporter you can talk to about how you can fulfill your potential—who you can email, complain to, and voice your concerns to—you'll be fine! I promise.

Stop waiting for everyone else to come around and support your dreams. Start working on your dreams, and the haters, the complainers and the doubters will eventually come around.

Whatever you do in life, people will complain or disagree with you. For example, in every set of student evaluations that I receive for a course, I'll get the most glowing compliments for how much direction I give for assignments, and at the same time other students complain that I waste time going over assignment instructions. You can't win them all.

You must believe in yourself and visualize yourself succeeding in life. Visualize that ultimate dream for yourself becoming a reality.

Lean on your ONE supporter for help, guidance and camaraderie.

Then WORK YOUR BUTT OFF in order to achieve greatness.

Accept whatever your situation is right now. Accept that maybe your friends don't think you'll ever get to graduate school, or that your family wants you to be a doctor but you hate medicine—and are too scared to tell them. Accept that you're not quite there yet . . . and then *DO WHATEVER IS NECESSARY TO ACHIEVE SUCCESS.*

Accept the present for what it is. Work towards your future . . . because it's bright.

Reference Letter Etiquette
(for Students)

You need only one kind of reference letter: A GREAT ONE. Anything else is a waste of time.

So how do you get a great letter of reference from one of your professors?

- *STAND OUT FROM THE CROWD!* Professors interact with hundreds, sometimes thousands of students a year, and everyone wants a letter of reference. But only a select few will get great letters. You must get to know your instructors well, so they know you by name (not just recognize your face):
  - o   Introduce yourself during the first class.
  - o   Ask questions during lectures. This is a good way to distinguish yourself from others.
  - o   Speak to your instructors after class.
  - o   Send them an idea for a lecture (an interesting video or news story).
  - o   Ask a question about a reading.
  - o   Volunteer during class discussions.
  - o   Always, always, *always* see your professors during their office hours! —This is a must. This is your one opportunity for individualized attention, even if it's just for eight minutes.
  - o   Ask for feedback on your assignments—how you can improve your work, your writing, or your critical analysis.
  - o   Lean into your education and take every opportunity to stand out from the crowd by being positive and energetic.
- *ASK THE RIGHT PERSON!* The right person is the one who knows you and your work the best. You need to establish a

relationship BEFORE you ask for a letter of reference. The more courses you take with the same professor the better.

- *DESERVE A GREAT LETTER OF REFERENCE!* Are you an exceptional student? Is your writing phenomenal? Are you active and present during lecture? Have I seen growth in your work? Are you dedicated to improving yourself? Do you have an unbelievable work ethic? Because if you're just average, then you'll just get an average letter of reference (if that).

- *ASK EARLY!* Give your instructors every opportunity to write you the best possible reference letter. That means giving them lots of time—preferably weeks in advance. Ask early and if they say "yes," then remind them of the due dates periodically.

- *HOW TO ASK.* It's simple: "Would you be willing to write me a GREAT letter of reference?" Remember, you're not looking for an average letter—you want a great one. If the instructor doesn't think they can provide you with a great letter, move on.

Tips on Reference Letters
(for Students)

If someone has agreed to write you a letter of reference, then it's your job to make their life easier by providing all the necessary information.

WHAT TO PROVIDE YOUR REFEREES WITH

- *What* are you applying for? (Name of program, department or school.)
- *Why* are you applying? Why are you a good candidate for this position? (Write this in ONE paragraph.)
- *Details* about yourself (awards, volunteer work, languages spoken, high grades received, dean's list or honor roll, classes you've taken with the referee, anything else interesting or unique about yourself).
- Provide a *statement of interest* (this is usually part of your application package already. It's also called a "personal statement").
- Your *transcripts.*
- Your *resume/CV.*
- *Sample of your best writing* (preferably from the instructor's course).
- *Anything else* you want specifically mentioned (for instance, maybe it's important to emphasize volunteer work or your time management or public speaking skills). Tell us what you would like emphasized. This matters.
- *Names* (who are we addressing the letter to?) and *dates* (when is this due?).
- Remind us of the *deadlines* a few times. We have a lot going on in our lives, so don't feel like you're pestering us. Believe

me, the gentle reminders help, especially one week before they're due.

- *Send a thank-you email.* Common courtesy goes a long way.
- Finally, *keep in touch* and let us know what happened. Did you get in? We spent time writing a letter for you; we're invested, too. So let us know!

Job-Hunting:
You Need to Follow Up

A colleague of mine is hiring for a new sales position. He received 52 resumes. And not one person followed up with him! This is shocking to me. I asked him what he'll do with the resumes. He told me he had already thrown them all out: "Why would I make the effort to call them, when they haven't made the effort to follow up with me? It's just basic job-hunting stuff."

Yes, it is basic, but most people don't put in enough effort, time and dedication to get the job they want.

If the perfect job doesn't quite exist for you, then create it. Tweet an executive in the organization. Tell them your great idea and how you're a perfect fit for the job.

If you don't follow up, you're guaranteed not to get the job.

During tougher economic times, finding a job can be more difficult, so be creative, and think outside-of-the-box. Employers appreciate this.

After you've applied for a job, consider doing the following:

- *Drop by the company in person* (if possible) and AVOID the HR manager. Instead, speak directly with the hiring manager or owner. Try to bypass HR completely. Don't just speak to the administrative assistants. Make sure the decision-makers actually meet you.
- *Send an email and ask for the sale.* Ask when interviews are taking place. Then ask for an interview.
- *Call the manager on the phone* and ask personally when your interview is scheduled, or better yet, ask for the job.
- *Use Twitter or Facebook.* Almost all companies have Twitter now, so send a clever tweet out to the company and ask for an interview.
- *Reach out to your contacts.* Contact everyone you know on LinkedIn and Facebook, and find out if one of your contacts

knows someone in the company. Do a little bit of the Kevin-Bacon-six-degrees-of-separation thing. Who must you meet to get you to the person who will introduce you to a key decision maker?

- *Perfect your elevator pitch and "accidentally" run into the hiring manager.* Always have your elevator pitch ready. Know what your value is to the company and why others should be interested in you or hire you. Practice your elevator pitch so that when an opportunity arises, you'll maximize the moment, instead of squandering it.

- *Don't ever think that minimal amounts of effort will get you success.* If you put in just the bare minimum, just the average amount of work, then average results are what you'll get.

Stop wasting time on creating the perfect resume or cover letter. Start figuring out how to get in front of the manager or decision-makers, then impress them with your enthusiasm, passion and eagerness to learn.

Before the Job Interview

Do your homework! You must research the company. Know what they do, what they stand for and, more importantly, what value you can add to the company. Know their products, their competition and the names of the top leadership. Know their successes and failures. And make sure they know you know it! Tie in a surprising fact or statistic so that it shows you've done your homework. Do you know who will be interviewing you? Find out and then do a little research on them. You need to be able to speak knowledgeably about the company in order to create the idea that you're a good fit.

Assess your social media presence. When employers Google your name (and they will!), what will they find? Photos of you drinking beer? Delete. Bikini shots? Delete. Selfie shots with a lot of cleavage? Delete. Your online photos are a representation of who you are and by extension the company or brand you work for. Remember that nothing is private anymore. If you get hired, you must make sure your social media presence will never embarrass the firm. Join LinkedIn and make sure you have a catchy or creative headline that immediately lets people know who you are and what you're interested in (for example, "Newly graduated sociologist with a contagious passion for gender studies"). Make sure all your social media outlets look professional and that your messaging is on-target and consistent across all platforms.

Develop your elevator pitch. This is so important, and it's shocking how many people have no idea what their elevator pitch is. You will miss out on crucial networking opportunities and chance meetings if you don't have a perfected elevator pitch. This is your 30- to 60-second chance to impress, get noticed and stand out from the crowd.

Bring copies of your resume/CV/cover letter. Always have extra copies on hand (literally in a file folder that's easily accessible). Don't go rummaging through your bag looking for a copy. You never want to make them wait. Look prepared and professional at all times. Make sure it's a clean copy that's not bent or crinkled. Also, bring copies of your list of references.

Prepare answers. Having a prepared answer to the most common interview questions is a basic prerequisite. Do not try to "ad lib" on the spot. Ever listen to wedding speeches that tried to just "wing it"? Brutal. They're the worst, and the person always sounds like an idiot. Write down your answers and practice saying them aloud. Then practice in front of others. You never want a situation where you've thought of the best answer AFTER the interview. Be prepared, sound prepared. You need to convince the employer you're the perfect candidate for the job, especially if you don't have all the required experience or education. It's your job to draw the connections between you and the job, not the employer's.

Prepare questions of your own. Always prepare a few thoughtful questions (no more than three or four) to ask your potential employer. This shows initiative and professionalism. You will be asked at the end of the interview if you have any questions. Count on this. It always happens, so prepare for it.

Prepare for different types of interview formats. You'll always be told in advance what type of interview it is. If not, make sure you ask so that you can prepare. It could be a panel interview, a group interview, a mock-lecture interview or telephone interview. Know the type and prepare for it.

Practice, practice, practice. The single most important thing you can do before your interview is to practice every aspect of it. Practice your handshake (see the chapter on this); practice how you'll introduce yourself and provide a sound bite or tag line (see the chapter on that); practice how you'll sound answering the questions. Shoot a video of yourself and assess your tone, mannerisms and facial expressions. Practice your answers. Practice your closing statement and goodbye. Practice it all.

Common Interview Questions

You need to prepare answers to the most commonly asked interview questions, so that you're never surprised or caught off guard. Be prepared as well to discuss anything on your resume or cover letter. It's all fair game.

1. What are your strengths?
2. What are your weaknesses?
3. Why do you want to work for us?
4. Why do you want to work in this field?
5. Why are you a good fit for this company?
6. Why did you leave your previous job?
7. Tell us about the most recent time you faced a challenge at work and how you handled it.
8. What experiences have you had in a leadership position?
9. Describe a situation where you mishandled people. How did you get through it? What did you learn?
10. Tell me about yourself.
11. What are your short- and long-term goals? Where do you see yourself a year from now? Five years from now?
12. What is your favorite book? [Or:] What's the last book you read?
13. What newspapers or magazines do you read?
14. What websites do you visit?
15. What Twitter/Pinterest/Instagram accounts do you follow?
16. What are your hobbies or interests outside of work?
17. Do you have any questions? (YES! Make sure you have questions prepared to ask your potential employer.)
18. What value do you bring to this company?
19. What was your most/least challenging job? Why?
20. Who do you admire most and why?
21. What do you regret not doing with your life (yet)?
22. How have you been successful in the past?
23. Describe what failure means to you.

24. How would your previous employer [or your professors, if still at school] describe you?
25. Tell me how you researched our company.
26. What's your purpose in life or vision for your life?
27. Give me a 60-second pitch for this company. Pretend I'm a potential client and you need to sell me the company's products and services.
28. Tell me about an important decision you made in the past year. How did you come to this decision and why?
29. What was the worst manager or worst job you ever had? Why?
30. What was the best manager or best job you ever had? Why?

Prepare for these types of questions by reading books and websites about interviewing techniques, writing down your answers, recording your answers on your smart phone, and doing mock interviews with your family and friends. *You can never be TOO prepared for a job interview.*

During the Interview

Interviews are about three things: (1) Do you have the skills and experience necessary to do the job? (2) Are you a good person to work with (no one wants to work with a jerk); and, most importantly, (3) PROMOTING YOURSELF. Focus on what you can do for the company, not just what you've done in the past.

Punctuality matters. DO NOT BE LATE. This is a serious mistake that's usually impossible to recover from. First impressions matter. Showing up late to an interview indicates you're irresponsible, you don't value other people's time and you're disorganized. No one cares why you were late. All that matters is that you were late.

Be friendly and polite with everyone. Making a good first impression starts from the moment you walk into the building. Be polite with everyone, not only because it's the right thing to do, but also because employers hire people they like—people they genuinely want to work with.

Dress for success. Always dress professionally for an interview. I would err on the more conservative side, but still showcase your personality. When in doubt, always dress up, not down. It's always better to be over-dressed than to look like a schlep.

Avoid fragrance. Now that more offices and businesses have fragrance-free policies, you should steer clear of any offending scents. Avoid overwhelming your potential employer with your "ocean spray" deodorant, your "summer breeze" hairspray, your perfume, your coco butter hand cream, etc. Choose a scent-free option for all your toiletries.

For smokers. Do not show up to the interview reeking of smoke. It's gross. Enough said. If you have to smoke beforehand, make sure you've brushed your teeth, used mouthwash, washed your hands and sprayed an air-freshener on your clothes. Non-smokers can smell cigarette smoke a mile away. Don't offend your employer before you've even had a chance to speak.

Have a strong handshake. Make sure your hands are dry, offer your hand, shake hands with a firm grip, smile and maintain eye contact. Never, ever offer one of those limp handshakes. Nothing says you lack confidence more than a weak handshake.

Check your body language. Make eye contact! This is so important and speaks to your confidence level. How do you sit in a chair? Leaning backward (signals boredom)? Arms crossed (you're angry and resentful)? Leaning forward (YES! It projects confidence and interest)? Be aware of what your body language says to others.

Promote yourself. This is not the place to be humble or shy. Don't talk about what a team player you are. You need to sell yourself and your skills. Make it memorable. Have a prepared "elevator pitch," and showcase what you can bring to the company. Don't just list all your attributes or skills or talk about what you did in the past. I know how uncomfortable this makes most women, but you must practice promoting yourself, because if you don't sing your own praises, you can absolutely, without a doubt, bet that NO ONE ELSE will.

Ask for the sale—finish strong. Ask for the job. Why else are you there? You're there to get the job! You're there to fill a gap with your own unique skills and experiences.

Ask questions! See the next chapter.

Best Questions to Ask in Your Interview

An interview serves two main purposes: (1) to figure out if you're the right candidate for the position; and (2) to figure out if the company is the right employer for you.

You should come prepared with your own list of questions in order to effectively figure out if this company is the right place for you. Asking the right questions also demonstrates your enthusiasm for the company.

Never ask about salary, benefits, vacation time, flex time or weekends off during the first interview, or else there won't be a second one. Also avoid asking any questions that are easily answered on the company website or through a basic Google search.

1. Why is this position vacant? Why did the last person leave this position?
2. What's the biggest problem that your staff faces? How could I help the situation?
3. What do you enjoy or appreciate the most about working for this company? (i.e. company culture)
4. Please explain the organizational structure of the company.
5. What are my daily responsibilities in this position? What will be expected of me?
6. What are the most challenging aspects of this position?
7. Compared to the competition, what are some of the company's core strengths and weaknesses?
8. How will my performance be evaluated (on what criteria) and how often?
9. How do you train and develop your employees? Is there a formal training program?
10. What is the average work week expected to be here?

If you really want to stand out from the crowd, you can ask more creative questions, such as:

1. Have I said anything during this interview that makes you think I'm not the perfect candidate for this position?
2. What weaknesses do you think I have? Do you see any gaps in my qualifications?
3. Is there any reason why I shouldn't be hired today?
4. Why don't you hire me today?

After the Interview

- *Send a thank-you note.* Immediately after the interview, make sure you've written down the names of everyone who interviewed you (better still, make sure you got their business cards), and send a thank-you email within 24 hours. Don't just say *"I'd love the opportunity to work for your company."* That sounds lame. Everyone else says that. Stand out by stating WHAT VALUE you bring to the company. Include something from the interview in the email.

- *Follow up.* If you don't hear anything within a week, send another courteous email or make a phone call.

- *If you don't get the job, try to find out why.* Be open to feedback. Ask if they have any advice or suggestions on how your interview could have been improved.

- *Don't internalize your failures.* Easier said than done, I know. Remember that research shows men externalize their failures while women internalize them. More men apply for leadership positions; therefore, more men achieve leadership positions. They're just MORE willing to get rejected, in order to eventually get a win.[78] Internalization will only keep you locked in a negative head-space. Regroup, reframe and re-charge. You didn't get the job? Move on.

- *Put in 10 times the effort you think necessary.* Most people send off a few resumes, get a handful of job interviews and think they're done. You must be prepared to WORK harder than anyone else to get a job! Don't count on getting that one particular job either. Make sure you have multiple job interviews on the go, so that if one doesn't pan out, you can still pay your bills next month.

How to Negotiate Your Salary

WHY WOMEN DON'T NEGOTIATE

We're nurturers, right? We're not supposed to be warriors, looking out for ourselves. We're taught to be nice, play by the rules, and wait our turn. Sadly, our turn never came and no one told us we didn't need to ask permission to want more out of life.

WHY WOMEN NEED TO NEGOTIATE

Men have always made more than women. This is not news. But things aren't getting better. Even though women earn more post-secondary degrees than men, in Ontario we make 72 cents for every dollar a man makes.[79] Yikes! In the U.S., with the same educational background (right out of college), women make 82 cents for every dollar a man makes doing the same work.[80]

For instance, in Lena Dunham's *Lenny Letter* e-newsletter, actress Jennifer Lawrence recently wrote about how the Sony hack revealed her failed negotiation tactics. *"When I found out how much less I was being paid than the lucky people with dicks, I didn't get mad at Sony.*

> **I got mad at myself. I failed as a negotiator because I gave up early.**
> —*Jennifer Lawrence, actress*

I got mad at myself. I failed as a negotiator because I gave up early." And why didn't she negotiate for more money? Because of FEAR! She goes on to say: *"I didn't want to seem 'difficult' or 'spoiled.' At the time, that seemed like a fine idea, until I saw the payroll on the Internet and realized every man I was working with definitely didn't worry about being 'difficult' or 'spoiled.'"*[81]

Unlike Jennifer Lawrence, most of us aren't negotiating for millions of dollars. But that fact makes effective negotiation even more important. So, before you sign your next job contract, please read through these tips.

TIPS

- *Never discuss compensation until you've been offered the job.*
- *Never sign anything the day you receive it.* Everyone expects that you'll take a day or two to read it over. If you can afford it, have a lawyer look at it; at the very least, run it by someone else whose opinion you respect.
- *Never accept the first offer.* Always counteroffer. You can also counteroffer on issues other than base salary. What about bonuses, perks, vacation time, health insurance, flex time, gas mileage and travel expenses, per diems, commissions, training opportunities, or tuition reimbursement?
- *Never say you need to speak to your spouse about it.* Honestly, if you can't make a decision without consulting your spouse, the company probably doesn't want you. I know this sounds harsh, but women always say this, and men never do. Even if it's true (of course you want to discuss things with your spouse!), don't say it. You should sound like you make your own decisions.
- *Do your homework.* You must know what the average salary is for someone of your related skills and experience. You've got to have a reference point for why you're asking for a certain amount. Be prepared to justify your price point on grounds other than "Mama needs new shoes." Although you always want to ask for more, be careful you don't price yourself out of the running for the job by an unrealistically or unreasonably high figure.
- *What's your walk-away point?* You need to know your absolute lowest acceptable offer. What are you not willing to work for? That's your walk-away point. Be prepared to walk if the salary or conditions aren't suitable. You don't have to accept the job; you can turn it down. —Easier said than done if

you really need the income. But being underpaid will start to grate on you eventually. If you really need the job and there's nothing else out there for now, still negotiate, still try to get more than the original offer.

- Recognize that gendered ideas about how women should act still exist. Women are still perceived as "demanding" or "aggressive" if they negotiate, while it's totally expected of men. Research shows that during negotiations, women should smile, be friendly, and show concern for the company first. I know, it's gross! Sheryl Sandberg also recommends substituting "we" for "I."[82]

How to Negotiate a Raise or Promotion

Here's how women typically start negotiations: "I'm sorry to spring this on you, I'm not sure if this is a good time or not, but I was wondering if we could possibly talk about my salary. It's not that I don't love working here, and I'm really grateful for all the opportunities I've had here, it's just that daycare is expensive, and I haven't had a salary increase in a few years, and I was hoping you could help me out a little. Do you think I could maybe get a raise this year?"

Here's how someone who's confident would start negotiations: "Based on the contributions and value I've added to the company over the past year, [such as . . .], I'm underpaid."

Oh. My. Gawd. Do you see the difference?

The woman begins with an apology, drones on and on, is tentative, unsure, and never mentions her contributions, then ends with a yes-or-no question. So the answer to her request for a raise is easy: "No."

Don't be this woman. Come prepared, be confident, and know your value.

TIPS

- *You must always self-promote!* This is the most important yet most difficult step for women. Women HATE self-promotion; they hate singing their own praises because it feels cocky, overly confident or boastful. If you don't let others know of your accomplishments on a regular basis, you will continue to be outplayed, out-salaried and out-maneuvered by others.

- *Schedule a meeting* with your boss with the stated intention of discussing your contributions to the company and compensation. That way both parties know exactly what to expect in the meeting. Do not wait for your annual review to ask for your raise. Ask beforehand.

- *Do your homework!* Suze Orman recommends that you pre-pare a one-page document (no longer) that describes your contributions to the company.[83] Give this to your boss a few days before your scheduled meeting. It's more difficult to reject a request for a raise when you've backed up your points with research and facts.

- *Know what you want.* Do you know exactly what you're asking for? Be clear. Are you asking for a salary increase, a bonus, an assistant, stock options, a bigger office, or a better title? You need to be completely sure of what you want or else you'll get steamrolled in the negotiations and leave with nothing.

- *Come prepared* to the meeting with a list of accomplishments. Know your accomplishments well and be able to speak about the value you add to the company.

- *Always ask for more!* Always. It's part of basic negotiating strategies. People expect that you'll ask for more, and you can expect that your boss will offer less. That's how it goes. Money is powerful and if you don't ask for more money right now, then you will feel the cumulative effects years later when you can't retire or afford a vacation or, worse yet, can't afford to walk away from a toxic work environment. You must always ask for more.

- *Keep your emotions out of the office!* You must stick to the facts. This is a business transaction. There's nothing personal about it, so don't bring the personal into it.

- *Do not cry* if your request for a raise gets rejected. What else can you negotiate? Flex time, more vacation time, a shorter work day, more responsibility at work, or different projects? Do not leave that office without something gained, or else it will be a defeating and deflating experience for you.

- *Realize that a raise isn't an automatic feature built into jobs.* Sometimes people expect a raise because they've worked hard, or have been there for a year, or haven't had a raise in a year. And actually, none of these reasons matter. The only thing that matters is results. Did you get results for your company? *A raise isn't automatic.* Read that last sentence again. RESULTS are expected. Keep adding value and making contributions to your company and you'll be duly compensated.[84]

- *Practice.* If you don't think you can wing it during the negotiation meeting, then look in the mirror and say your pitch. Ask a friend to role play with you as you go through objections. Have your counter-arguments ready to meet any objections. This will better prepare you for the actual meeting. Ask with confidence, and if you don't have a lot of confidence, then fake it! (And keep practicing.)

- *Never start negotiations by apologizing for taking up time.* Stop apologizing! The absolute worst time to apologize is at the beginning of a negotiation. It sets the wrong tone: You come across as meek, tentative, and unsure of yourself. Why would you apologize? You booked the meeting ahead of time, your boss knows why you're meeting, you're prepared, and you're not wasting anyone's time. Kick yourself the next time you apologize. Ugh. Enough said.

- *Ask for something specific.* Don't ask yes-or-no questions. Avoid asking "Can I have a raise?" —No, you can't. Case closed. Now what do you do? Instead, always give your boss a choice: "I'd be willing to accept a 5% or 6% increase; what do you think?"

- *If you hear "no" or get rejected—PERSIST.* This is a deal-breaker. Women walk away after the first "no," while men are just getting warmed up. Your boss will perceive you differently if you walk away without a fight rather than persisting and coming at the objection in different ways. In negotiations, you're perceived either as weak and easy to say "no" to, OR someone who is confident and knows their value. Confidence always wins out.

- *Keep this in mind:* Men negotiate up to four times more often than women. When women do negotiate their salary, they ask for 30% less than their male counterparts.[85]

I want every little
girl who's told she's
"bossy"
to be told instead
that she has leader-
ship skills.

— *Sheryl Sandberg,*
CEO, FaceBook

7

Conclusion

We Need to Build a Coalition!

I know our "responsibilities" as women are endless (worker, financial planner, mother, parent, chef, nutritionist, appointment-maker, cleaner, organizer, dog walker, family-event planner, spouse, lover, friend, "soulmate," stylist, allergist, and family enthusiast), but I need to add one more item to this list.

We need to build a coalition of strong, empowered, confident women. And I need your help.

Once you've begun your journey of increasing your assertiveness and your confidence, reach out to other women. Help them out. Encourage them.

Once you've mastered your public speaking, communication or negotiation skills, look to help other women: your neighbours, sisters, spouses, daughters, friends and business associates.

We are in this together.

We must be there for each other.

We must draw strength and encouragement from one another's success. One woman's success does not negate our own. There is room for all of us to be successful, as long as you're willing to work harder for it than anyone else.

Be a role model. Be a mentor. Let's create a coalition, a movement of women reaching UP. Reach UP for leadership positions. Reach UP for success.

Don't hang out with the mediocre. Don't let "averageness" into your life.

Expect more from yourself and those in your life.

Let's change the statistics on women leaders in the world. Please let's start supporting and encouraging other women to reach for success.

Every time someone tells me how assertive my daughter is, I think, "Cool, then I'm raising her well." Seriously. I'm not raising a doormat, I'm not raising a follower. I'm raising a leader. I AM RAISING A QUEEN.

That's what I want for women. I want them to lead. I want them to *want* to lead, and believe they are worthy of leadership positions.

I want our daughters, our sisters, our colleagues—all of us—*to see opportunities for negotiation and success everywhere.*

> I just love bossy women. I could be around them all day. To me, bossy is not a pejorative term at all. It means somebody is passionate and engaged and ambitious, and doesn't mind leading.
>
> —Amy Poehler

I want us to push beyond our comfort zones and reach for MORE, reach UP. Success must be our only option.

I want dinner parties where we talk about self-promotion and self-advocacy instead of yet another celebrity cookbook or reality star scandal!

I want conversations with women where no one mentions diet or their body weight, and instead we talk about our careers and our financial situation (as in, how can we make more $$$?!).

This is what I want for women.

This is what I want for my daughter.

This is what I want for myself.

This is why we need more bossy women who aren't afraid of voicing their opinions, speaking aloud, asking for what they want and who will negotiate for themselves.

ALL. THE. TIME.

LET'S BE BOSSY WOMEN TOGETHER.

THANK YOU.

Acknowledgements

I'd like to start off by thanking myself! Damn, girl, you did it! I had a vision, I had a plan, and then I WORKED that plan, every damn day.

To my ALL IN club members, thank you for taking a chance on me and this club. Thank you for jumping out of your comfort zone and practicing those public speaking drills. Now look at you!

To my blog readers, thank you for reading and commenting. Your support helped push this book through.

To my students, thank you for your encouragement and your feedback on the struggles and fears women face in school and beyond.

Thank you to my research assistants: Charnjot Ghuman, Alyson McLeod, Carly McLeod, and Melanie Pohl, for your invaluable insight, dedication to the ALL IN message and your continued support. Your constructive feedback matters to me.

To my editor David Stover at Rock's Mills Press, thank you so much for believing in me and this message of empowerment. Thank you for supporting my ability to articulate these ideas in a different, out-of-the-box format. You helped bring my first book to fruition!

To my husband Steve, who pushed me off the ledge and demanded greatness of me.

To my daughter Ryo. I hope you know the possibilities for greatness reside within. I hope that the process of watching me write this book has shown you the power of hard work, and the beautiful consequences of persistent, deliberate and focused effort. I hope you realize that Mama banned princesses from the house so that you would learn to rely on your own skills and talents to succeed in life, and not wait for someone to save you, rescue you, pay your bills, or "complete" you. There is only you, and you must always reach UP and demand more of yourself.

Finally, to my parents Lillian and Walter Jovanović. My mother is my mentor and an indisputable example of a strong, capable, confident, and utterly fear-
less woman. I learned, I absorbed, and I emulated your excellence throughout my life. My father's work ethic showed me that work-ing 70 hours a week was the only way to get your dreams.

> **Option A is not available. So let's kick the sh** out of Option B.**
> —*Sheryl Sandberg*

He took care of our family so my mother and I could keep earning all these degrees! My quest for greatness began at home. It began when I got an A and you wanted to know what happened to the A+. It began when I wanted to be a lawyer and you said, "Why not prime minister?" You instilled in me the idea that I was capable of anything, but only if I outworked everyone else, only if the end product was extraordinary. This is my end product—it just took me longer than expected to get here. I hope I make you proud. You are my tiger parents, and I wouldn't have it any other way.

About the Author

Professor Maja Jovanović is the founder and CEO of ALL IN Enterprises, a company that gives women the tools and strategies they need to become leaders in all areas of their lives.

Prof. Maja, as she's known, created ALL IN as a way to help women turn their fears into success. Professor Maja is a medical sociologist, researcher, writer and public speaker. This is her first book.

Prof. Maja earned her master's degree in sociology from the University of Waterloo and her Ph.D., also in sociology, from McMaster University, where she currently teaches. Her main interests are female empowerment and confidence issues, along with health and nutrition and body positivity. She is also a holistic nutritionist and a vegan. She's an avid runner (when not nursing an injury) and Great Dane owner. She lives near Toronto, with her husband Steve, their daughter Ryo and their Great Dane Cooper.

Stay connected with Prof. Maja through her blog (http://allinwithprofmaja.com) and YouTube Channel. Contact her by leaving comments on her blog or emailing her at allinwith-maja@gmail.com.

ADDITIONAL RESOURCES
Books I Love

Here is a list of some of my favorite books—the ones that inspire me, make me laugh, and force me to re-think my work habits. Each has been useful, insightful and motivating in its own way.

Mika Brzezinski, *Knowing Your Value: Women, Money and Getting What You're Worth*. New York: Weinstein Publishing, 2012.

Grant Cardone, *The 10X Rule: The Only Difference between Success and Failure*. Hoboken, NJ: Wiley, 2014.

Arlene Dickinson, *Persuasion*. Toronto: Collins, 2011.

Arlene Dickinson, *All In: You, Your Business, Your Life*. Toronto: Collins, 2013.

Fredrik Eklund, *The Sell: The Secrets of Selling Anything to Anyone*. New York: Penguin Random House, 2015.

T.S. Eliot, *Selected Poems*. London: Faber, 1954.

Karen Finerman, *Finerman's Rules: Secrets I'd Only Tell My Daughters about Business and Life*. New York: Business Plus, 2013.

Emma Forrest, *Your Voice in My Head: A Memoir*. Toronto: Random House Canada, 2011.

Lois Frankel, *Nice Girls Don't Get The Corner Office: Unconscious Mistakes Women Make that Sabotage Their Careers*. Revised edition. New York: Business Plus, 2014.

Judith Humphrey, *Taking the Stage: How Women Can Speak Up, Stand Out, and Succeed*. Hoboken, NJ: Wiley Jossey-Bass, 2015.

Mindy Kaling, *Why Not Me?* New York: Crown Archetype, 2015.

Brian Moran and Michael Lennington, *The 12 Week Year: Get More Done in 12 Weeks than Others Do in 12 Months*. Hoboken, NJ: Wiley, 2013.

Bill McGowan, *Pitch Perfect: How to Say it Right the First Time, Every Time*. New York: HarperBusiness, 2014.

Amy Poehler, *Yes, Please*. New York: HarperCollins, 2014.

Steven Pressfield, *Do the Work.* New York: Black Irish Entertainment, 2015.

Steven Pressfield, *Turning Pro: Tap Your Inner Power and Create Your Life's Work.* New York: Black Irish Entertainment, 2012.

Steven Pressfield, *The War of Art: Break through the Blocks and Win Your Inner Creative Battles.* New York: Black Irish Entertainment, 2002.

Ronda Rousey, *Rousey: My Fight/Your Fight.* New York: Regan Arts, 2015.

Joan Rivers, *Diary of a Mad Diva.* New York: Berkley Publishing, 2014.

Joan Rivers, *I Hate Everyone . . . Starting with Me.* New York: Berkley Publishing, 2012.

Melissa Rivers, *The Book of Joan: Tales of Mirth, Mischief and Manipulation.* New York: Crown Publishing. 2015.

Sheryl Sandberg, *Lean In: Women, Work and the Will to Lead.* New York: Knopf, 2013.

Sheryl Sandberg, *Lean In for Graduates.* New York: Knopf, 2014.

Selena Rezvani, *Pushback: How Smart Women Ask and Stand Up for What They Want.* San Francisco: Wiley, 2012.

Eckhart Tolle, *A New Earth: Awakening to Your Life's Purpose.* New York: Dutton, 2005.

Eckhart Tolle, *The Power of Now: A Guide to Spiritual Enlightenment.* Vancouver, BC: Namaste Publishing, 2004.

Kim Thuy, *RU.* Toronto: Vintage Canada, 2012. (2015 Canada Reads winner.)

Ivanka Trump, *The Trump Card: Playing to Win in Work and Life.* New York: Touchstone Books, 2010.

Jessica Valenti, *Full Frontal Feminism: A Young Woman's Guide to Why Feminism Matters*, 2nd edition. Berkeley, CA: Seal Press, 2014.

Notes

1. Sheryl Sandberg, *Lean In: Women, Work and the Will to Lead* (New York: Knopf, 2013).
2. Retrieved from https://www.whitehouse.gov/issues/equal-pay and https://www.whitehouse.gov/blog/2015/04/14/five-facts-about-gender-pay-gap.
3. "Catalyst Accord: Women on Corporate Boards in Canada," retrieved from http://www.catalyst.org/catalyst-accord-women-corporate-boards-canada. See also OECD, Closing the Gender Gap: ACT NOW, retrieved from http://www.keepeek.com/Digital-Asset-Management/oecd/social-issues-migration-health/close-the-gender-gap-now_9789264179370-en#page7.
4. For the Geena Davis Institute on Gender in Media website see: http://seejane.org/.
5. For the executive summary of the report "Gender Bias Without Borders" (2014) see: http://seejane.org/wp-content/uploads/gender-bias-without-borders-executive-summary.pdf.
6. See the report: "Occupational Aspirations: What are Films Teaching About the World of Work?" (2010) http://seejane.org/wp-content/uploads/key-findings-occupational-aspirations-2013.pdf.
7. See the report "Occupational Aspirations: What Are Films Teaching about the World of Work?" (2010) at http://seejane.org/wp-content/uploads/key-findings-occupational-aspirations-2013.pdf.
8. See the brilliant book *Rosie Revere, Engineer* (2013) by Andrea Beaty and David Roberts
9. Kate McInturff and Paul Tulloch, *Narrowing the Gap: The Difference that Public Sector Wages Make* (N.p.: Canadian Centre for Policy Alternatives, 2014).
10. See Statistics Canada's Report "Perspectives on Labour and Income: Returning to the Job after Childbirth," December 2007, by Xuelin Zhang, at http://www.statcan.gc.ca/pub/75-001-x/2007112/article/4096932-eng.htm.
11. "Is Breastfeeding Truly Cost Free? Income Consequences of Breastfeeding for Women" by Phyllis L. F. Rippeyounga and Mary C. Noonanb, *American Sociological Review,* April 2012 (77:2), pp. 244–267.
12. See http://www.dominican.edu/academics/ahss/undergraduate-programs/psych/faculty/assets/gail-matthews/researchsummary2.pdf.
13. Brian P. Moran and Michael Lennington, *The 12 Week Year: Get More Done in 12 Weeks than Others Do in 12 Months* (Hoboken, NJ: Wiley, 2013). See also Gary Keller and Jay Papasan, *The One Thing : The Surprisingly Simple Truth behind Extraordinary Results* (Austin, TX: Bard Press, 2012).
14. Moran and Lennington, *The 12 Week Year.*
15. Fredrik Eklund, *The Sell: The Secrets of Selling Anything to Anyone* (New York: Avery, 2015), p. 51.
16. See http://www.statisticbrain.com/attention-span-statistics/.

17. W. Mischel et al. (1989), "Delay of gratification in children," *Science* (244): 933–938; B.J. Casey et al. (2011), "Behavioral and neural correlates of delay of gratification 40 years later," *Proceedings of the National Academy of Sciences* 108(36): 14998–15003.

18. Brown, *The Gifts of Imperfection*, pp. 56–57.

19. Ibid.

20. See Grant Cardone, *The 10X Rule: The Only Difference Between Success and Failure* (Hoboken, NJ: Wiley, 2011).

21. Steven Pressfield, *The War of Art: Break Through the Blocks and Win Your Inner Creative Battles* (New York: Black Irish Entertainment, 2002), p. 8.

22. Ibid., p. 9.

23. See http://self-compassion.org/the-three-elements-of-self-compassion-2/.

24. Brown, *The Gifts of Imperfection*.

25. Georges Desvaux, Sandrine Devillard-Hoellinger, and Mary C. Meaney, "A Business Case for Women," *The McKinsey Quarterly*, 4 (September 2008). For a critique of the HP study and its wide dissemination, see Curt Rice's opinion piece at http://curt-rice.com/2014/04/22/what-happens-when-under-qualified-women-apply-for-jobs-and-why-sheryl-sandberg-and-mckinsey-wrongly-think-we-dont-know/.

26. Pew Research Center, January 2014, "E-Reading Rises as Device Ownership Jumps." Retrieved from http://pewinternet.org/Reports/2014 /E-Reading-Update.aspx.

27. http://www.harrypotter.bloomsbury.com/uk/jk-rowling-biography.

28. http://www.forbes.com/profile/sara-blakely/.

29. Arlene Dickinson, *All In* (New York: HarperCollins, 2013).

30. http://www.cbj.ca/power_of_persuasion_the_inspirational_life _story_of_arlene_dicki/.

31. http://www.cbj.ca/jim_treliving_and_arlene_dickinson_ making_the_big_decision/.

32. http://www.huffingtonpost.com/2015/05/05/arianna-huffington-ecourse-thrive_n_7213034.html

33. http://www.nytimes.com/2015/07/05/magazine/arianna-huffingtons-improbable-insatiable-content-machine.html?_r=0.

34. Linda Babcock and Sara Laschever, Women Don't Ask: The High Cost of Avoiding Negotiation and Positive Strategies for Change (New York: Bantam Books, 2007).

35. Katty Kay and Claire Shipman, *The Confidence Code: The Science and Art of Self-Assurance—What Women Should Know* (New York: HarperBusiness, 2014).

36. Ibid.

37. Mimi Nichter, *Fat Talk: What Girls and Their Parents Say About Dieting* (Cambridge, MA: Harvard University Press, 2000).

38. Lauren Williams and John Germov, "Constructing the Female Body: Dieting, the Thin Ideal and Body Acceptance" in *A Sociology of Food and Nutrition: The Social Appetite*, 3rd edition (Melbourne, Australia: Oxford University Press, 2008), pp. 329–62).

39. http://content.time.com/time/nation/article/0,8599,2025345,00.html.

40. See 2012 articles by Renee Engeln in *Psychology of Women Quarterly* or *Sex Roles*.

41. http://www.dove.us/Social-Mission/campaign-for-real-beauty.aspx. See also http://www.dove.us/Our-Mission/Girls-Self-Esteem/Our-Research/default.aspx.

42. See the following books for examples of how ultra-successful women still have fear or are affected by the fraud or imposter syndrome: Mika Brzezinski, *Knowing Your Value: Women, Money and Getting What You're Worth* (New York: Weinstein Books, 2011); Sheryl Sandberg, *Lean In: Women, Work and the Will to Lead* (New York: Knopf, 2013); Katty Kay and Claire Shipman, *The Confidence Code: The Science and Art of Self-Assurance—What Women Should Know* (New York: HarperBusiness, 2014); Brené Brown, *The Gifts of Imperfection: Let Go of Who You Think You're Supposed to Be and Embrace Who You Are* (Center City, MN: Hazelden, 2010); Mindy Kaling, *Why Not Me?* (New York: Crown Archetype, 2015); Arlene Dickinson, *All In* (New York: HarperCollins, 2013).

43. Peggy McIntosh, *Feeling like a Fraud* (work in progress) (Wellesley, MA: Wellesley Centers for Women (WCW), paper no. 18), retrieved from http://isites.harvard.edu/fs/docs/icb.topic857636.files/Fraud%20I.pdf.

44. Richard R. Peterson, "A Re-evaluation of the Economic Consequences of Divorce," *American Sociological Review*, 61 (1996): 528–36.

45. http://www.thesecret.tv/about/Ronda-byrnes-biography/

46. Sandberg, *Lean In*.

47. Susan Nolen-Hoeksema, *Women Who Think Too Much: How To Break Free of Over-Thinking and Reclaim Your Life* (New York: Henry Holt, 2003), p. 9.

48. Ibid.

49. Joanna Barsh and Susie Cranston, *How Remarkable Women Lead: The Breakthrough Model for Work and Life* (New York: Crown Business, 2009).

50. Eckhart Tolle, *The Power of Now: A Guide to Spiritual Enlightenment* (Vancouver, BC: Namaste Publishing, 2004).

51. Ibid., p. 82.

52. This tip comes from Moran and Lennington, *The 12 Week Year*, p. 149.

53. See Cardone, *The 10X Rule*.

54. For inspiring talks watch (1) Tavi Gevinson on TEDX Teen; (2) Kayla Kearney "comes out" in high school assembly (https://www.youtube.com/watch?v=InN6btoB8x0); (3) Maya Angelou's eulogy for Coretta Scott King; (4) "Viola Davis Talks Hunger Is Initiative at Power of Women" (https://www.youtube.com/watch? v=AMtKz54UcxQ). Also see www.tedwomen.com.

55. See Sandberg, *Lean In*; Kay and Shipman, *Confidence Code*; or Babcock and Lascheer, *Women Don't Ask*.

56. Kimberley A. Daubman et al., "Gender and the Self-Presentation of Academic Achievement," *Sex Roles*, 27, 3–4 (1992): 187–204; Laurie Heatherington et al., "Two Investigations of Female Modesty in Achievement Situations," *Sex Roles*, 29, 11–12 (1993): 739–54; Heatherington et al., "How'd You Do on that Test? The Effects of Gender on Self-Presentation of Achievement to Vulnerable Men," *Sex Roles*, 45, 3–4 (2002): 161–77; Sylvia Beyer and Edward M. Bowden, "Gender Differences in Self-Presentation: Convergent Evidence form Three Measures of Accuracy and Bias," *Personality and Social Psychology Bulletin*, 23, 2 (1997): 157–72.

57. Sandberg, Lean In.

58. Pew Research Center, January 2014, "E-Reading Rises."

59. See Paywatch, 2014.

60. Gregory S. Berns, et al., "Short- and Long-Term Effects of a Novel on Connectivity in the Brain," *Brain Connectivity* 3 (November 6, 2013), DOI: 10.1089/brain.2013.0166.

61. P. Lally et al. (2010), "How are habits formed: Modelling habit formation in the real world," *European Journal of Social Psychology* 40: 998–1009.

62. http://www.salary.com/2013-wasting-time-at-work-survey/.

63. Lois P. Frankel, *Nice Girls Don't Get the Corner Office: Unconscious Mistakes Women Make That Sabotage Their Careers*, rev. ed. (N.p.: Business Plus, 2014).

64. Linda D. Swink, *Speak with Power and Grace: A Woman's Guide to Public Speaking* (New York: Skyhorse Publishing, 2014).

65. Bill McGowan and Alisa Bowman, *Pitch Perfect: How to Say It Right The First Time, Every Time* (New York: Harper Business, 2015).

66. The following tips on how to sit in a chair are based on (1) my own experiences in every meeting and conference I've ever attended; (2) Sandberg, *Lean In*; (3) Judith Humphrey, *Taking the Stage: How Women Can Speak Up, Stand Put, and Succeed* (San Francisco: Jossey-Bass, 2012) (4) McGowan, *Pitch Perfect*.

67. William F. Chaplin et al., "Handshaking, Gender, Personality and First Impressions," *Journal of Personality and Social Psychology*, 79, 1 (2000): 110–17.

68. Babcock and Laschever, *Women Don't Ask*.

69. Ibid.

70. See https://www8.gsb.columbia.edu/articles/node/801/Confidence%20Game.

71. Eklund, *The Sell*; Grant Cardone, *Sell or Be Sold: How to Get Your Way in Business and in Life* (New York: GreenLeaf Book Group Press, 2012); Jeffrey Gitomer, *21.5 Unbreakable Laws of Selling* (Austin, TX: Bard Press, 2013).

72. Cardone, *Sell or Be Sold*.

73. Aliza Licht, *Leave Your Mark: Land Your Dream Job. Kill It In Your Career. Rock Social Media* (New York: Grand Central Publishing, 2015), p. 196.

74. http://www.nytimes.com/2014/09/11/fashion/steve-jobs-apple-was-a-low-tech-parent.html.

75. http://www.huffingtonpost.com/2015/05/27/richard-prince-instagram_n_7452634.html.

76. John C. Maxwell, *Sometimes You Win, Sometimes You Learn: Life's Greatest Lessons are Gained from Our Losses* (New York: Center Street Inc., 2013).

77. Brzezinski, *Knowing Your Value*; Dickinson, *Persuasion*; Ivanka Trump, *The Trump Card: Playing to Win in Work and Life* (New York: Touchstone Books, 2009).

78. Joanna Barsh and Lareina Yee, *Unlocking the Full Potential of Women at Work* (New York: McKinsey and Co., 2012).

79. Mary Cornish, "A Growing Concern: Ontario's Growing Gender Pay Gap," Canadian Centre for Policy Alternatives, April 2014.

80. Sheryl Sandberg, *Lean In for Graduates* (New York: Knopf, 2014), p. 303.

81. http://us11.campaign-archive1.com/?u=a5b04a26aae05a24bc4efb63e&id=64e6f35176&e=fe292e1416#wage.

82. Sandberg, *Lean In For Graduates*, p. 303.

83. Brzezinski, *Knowing Your Value*.

84. Trump, *The Trump Card*, p. 169.

85. Babcock and Laschever, *Women Don't Ask*.

WALTHAM
PUBLIC LIBRARY

CPSIA information can be obtained at www.ICGtesting.com
Printed in the USA
LVOW10s1447150616

492730LV00001B/149/P